Landmark

Landmark

COTTAGES, CASTLES AND CURIOSITIES OF BRITAIN IN THE CARE OF THE LANDMARK TRUST

Text and Photography by
Derry Brabbs

with an introduction by Sir John Smith CH CBE,
founder of the Landmark Trust

Weidenfeld & Nicolson
London

First published in Great Britain in 1998 by Weidenfeld & Nicolson

A CIP catalogue record for this book is available from the British Library.

ISBN 0 297 822993

Designed by Paul Cooper

Printed and Bound in Italy

ENDPAPERS: VIEW OF THE COUNTRYSIDE SURROUNDING CLYTHA CASTLE
HALF TITLE: CASTLE OF PARK
TITLE PAGE: THE OLD LIGHT, LUNDY

Weidenfeld & Nicolson
The Orion Publishing Group
Orion House
5 Upper St Martin's Lane
London WC2H 9EA

PREFACE

Sunset's rays briefly lit up the Union flag fluttering down its mast, signalling the end of another day in my castle. For one week, I was commanding a giant fortress just off the coast of the Channel Island of Alderney. Having made a pathetic attempt at the 'Last Post' on the fort's bugle, I retired to the officers' quarters.

That was just one of many memorable moments I have spent in historic buildings restored by the Landmark Trust and available for rent as holiday homes, a number of which had faced certain demolition. As so many people have never even heard of the Trust, I wanted to 'blow the trumpet' for it in this book, with more success, I hope, than my efforts on the bugle.

The Landmark Trust was founded by Sir John Smith in 1965 and I would like to express my sincere thanks to him for writing the introduction, in which he explains more about the charity and how it came into being.

A Landmark Trust handbook details all the properties, but in alphabetical order only, so I have attempted to group them together here under appropriate chapter headings. The plan has almost worked, but it does have a few quirks, rather like the buildings themselves. From Penzance to the Scottish Highlands, Landmarks, as the buildings are known, can be found in most parts of Britain. A location map, together with practical notes on how to contact the Trust for further information, can be found at the back of this book.

I hope the photographs and brief descriptions of this extraordinarily diverse collection of buildings will encourage people to discover the Landmark Trust for themselves.

DERRY BRABBS

INTRODUCTION

by Sir John Smith CH CBE, founder of the Landmark Trust

The Landmark Trust began its work in 1965. By then most buildings of the highest architectural quality were already well looked after – though, of course, there were, as now, occasional scandals and crises. But very many minor buildings, put up with thought and care by skilled, intelligent people long ago, were disappearing all the time. Without this general background of good but lesser architecture the best buildings, well-preserved, would soon look as out of place 'as a diamond ring in the spaghetti'. The Society for the Preservation of Ancient Buildings had long been aware of this, but it was a pressure group only, as were almost all other amenity bodies except the National Trust. However, the National Trust, fully stretched, could not be expected to rescue minor buildings in distress, which often needed perseverance and money just as much as love. It therefore seemed to me that a body was required to tackle cases too desperate, troublesome or unfashionable for anyone else.

I also wanted more people to have the experience of living in a historic building. By sleeping under its roof people profit far more from a place than by looking at it only; they can study it at leisure, be there early and late, in all lights and weathers, and get the feel of its surroundings. It occurred to me that the sort of buildings we were going to tackle, no longer wanted for their original purpose, might be let to people for holidays. In that way a constant succession of different people could actually live, however briefly, in historic buildings of every age and style; and might go back home with an interest awakened that would grow, perhaps last them all their lives, while also helping our cause. To walk in and out of a house at will for a week or so, and to carry the key of the door in your pocket, is a stimulus more powerful than a mere ticket of admission for a brief tour.

The Landmark therefore set out to do two things at once, each with an equal priority – to rescue handsome buildings heading for destruction or decay, and to give as many people as possible the rewarding, even mildly elevating experience of occupying them and exploring their surroundings. I suppose I am primarily a buildings 'buff', and I am always surprised how keen I am that people should actually enjoy and benefit from travelling to our various places and staying in them. I attribute this to genes inherited from my mother, whose grandfather founded the YMCA and whose great-grandfather was Thomas Cook.

What guided our choice of buildings? Since we could not rescue everything and because of our twin aims, we restricted ourselves to buildings in at least part of which people could stay for short periods – to enjoy themselves, or to do or study something in particular. Such buildings, however, quite often formed part of a group, the whole of which we had to take on, for example, at Cromford or Peasenhall. So we soon had a number of long-term tenants, including tenants of small shops; I was anxious to preserve both. I was also an admirer of military and industrial buildings, then for the most part ignored or disliked.

We had to hunt for our first projects – by carrying out research and then approaching the owners. Fort Clonque, the House of Correction and Purton Green are examples of this, as is Stogursey Castle, which was so overgrown that it was invisible, even from the air. No one except adventurous schoolboys can have seen it for many years. Soon, however, people began to tell us of all too many buildings in trouble, and others were offered, given or bequeathed to us. We reckoned to take on five or six new projects a year, so that building work might be going on at twelve or fifteen places at once. How was all this paid for? Asking other people for money is a miserable, time-consuming business, which I was determined to avoid. By chance, three years before starting the Landmark, I had thought of a new way of raising funds for charity. I did my best to get the National Trust to try it, but without success; so I tried it myself and, to my surprise, it produced a cataract of gold, far more than the Landmark could spend. Alas, times have changed and the flow is now reduced to a trickle, but for thirty years the Landmark did not have to worry about money at all.

Most of the buildings we tackled needed a great deal doing to them. We aimed at work of the highest quality – and in this way tried to preserve skills as well as buildings – but we did not like our places to be in what Queen Victoria called 'a very high state of preservation'. It is not easy to combine good and lasting work with a restrained approach; and there was always a temptation, sometimes pressure, to make everything as 'good' as new while we were at it. This was most marked with derelict timber-framed buildings. To repair these ruins of wood and plaster, eaten away by English weather, is like patching a cobweb. The urge is often powerful to replace too much, but the result is a building which has lost all feeling and looks as miserable as a small boy cleaned up by a tough mother.

However, we did not wish to preserve our places as dead, museum objects. They were to be occupied by human beings, who cook and wash and use the rooms. Occasionally, therefore, we needed to make with care some alteration to a building, but we hoped that in so doing we added further to its history. We did not believe, as some 'preservationists' seem to do, that history is over, and that nothing should ever be changed again. Our aim was to have a building and it surroundings look as though everything had fallen naturally into place, so that visitors, on first seeing it, would feel it had been like that all the time. Sometimes a waspish person, especially on Lundy, would say, 'You don't seem to have done much here.' We viewed that as high praise.

In those days self-catering holidays were in general a downmarket affair, for those, apart from a few enthusiasts, who could not afford anything better. However, we fitted out our buildings just as we would for ourselves – not making them luxurious or smart, but as practical and comfortable as their nature allowed. We also took much trouble when furnishing them, aiming to please the eye and interest people without being at all extravagant; almost all the furniture was old and good, unpretentious and carefully chosen. Indeed we found ourselves rescuing furniture in distress as well as buildings, by buying (and repairing) just those plain, admirable pieces with which England used to abound, but which were being exported by the shipload. All the pictures, however humble, had some special reason for being there. We were trying to preserve and restore not only the buildings but also the outlook on life which created them.

We also provided each Landmark with those books which we thought an inquiring visitor would like to find there – books about the neighbourhood and works of literature with local associations – and an album of historical notes, plans and photographs, showing how the place was when we found it and what we had done with it. A stay in a Landmark was meant to be not just a holiday but a fresh window on life.

This recipe appeared to work and, without advertising at all, we gradually built up a following. People only recommended us to their friends if they thought they would enjoy it. As a result there were few complaints or disappointments, even if, as at Swarkestone Pavilion, it was necessary to walk across the roof to reach the bathroom. That was part of the experience. We reckoned to finish and make available five or six additional buildings

Ingestre Pavilion
Nr Tixall, Staffordshire

each year, and our clientele expanded to keep pace and fill them. Because we did not advertise, people felt they had made a discovery for themselves, were members of a little-known club. Who were they? We met them seldom. Once a year we used to have a Gathering, of our staff and some of the 'campers' (as we called our customers, following the example of Billy Butlin). For one of these occasions we engaged a juggler. When he had completed his act, he threw his eight or so balls in rapid succession, as jugglers do, to one of our customers in the audience – who caught them all. The juggler was amazed and declared that it had never happened before. 'I'm a juggler,' replied our customer.

In each Landmark we placed a logbook in which our visitors could write whatever they liked for the benefit of their successors. Here, released from the strait-jacket of daily life, they revealed great enterprise and imagination. They found and recorded the most fascinating things to see and do, of greater variety then ever we could have suggested to them. Others were content just to be there, giving their cars a rest as well as themselves; and a noble few came by public transport, which serves many of our places very adequately. Many returned, to the same Landmark or to others in succession, and it warmed the heart when they wrote, 'I dream of staying again in each and every one.' Though no party occupies a Landmark for more than a short time, the logbook links visitors with those who come before and after, and gives to them and to the places a sense of continuity. These logbooks reward us for our labours, and show what real pleasure people, given half a chance, can still find in our battered island.

Those who care about their surroundings fight under a handicap. When a fine building is demolished or a fine place spoilt, that is the end of the matter; but the Vandal, even if driven off, can always try again. To win at all we have to win every time, whereas the forces of destruction need win but once. We are inevitably on the defensive, appearing to fight a rearguard action only; and it is all too easy for those who destroy to represent those who care as backward-looking and obstructive. But the reverse is the truth. Material progress has at least meant that we no longer have to foul our surroundings in order to survive. Indeed, it now seems that we cannot survive if we do. It is those who still preach cheapness at any price who are out of date; while those who preach against waste, whether of buildings or of other resources, are modern. Far from being something restrictive, preservation is now constructive, and creative as well. Those who care about the environment are, in fact, in the vanguard of progress and part of a growing army.

Moreover, the Landmark Trust is not just engaged in preservation. It is trying to make preservation unnecessary by opening the eyes of as many people as possible to what is being done to this country. Indeed our aim is to rouse people's interest in their surroundings in the widest sense – their surroundings both in space and time. The environment is not just a film set, as so many in the 'heritage industry' now regard it. History is part of our environment; so is the way people live, their scale of values, and how they treat each other and the rest of creation. We shall not, of course, attain these grandiose objectives, but if we can just nudge the cannonball of progress in its flight, then we shall be content. We hope that every day some of our many guests, as they set up house in one or other of our places, will feel that, as Bunyan said, 'here a man may be thinking what he is, whence he came, what he has done, and to what the King has called him.'

CASTLES, FORTS AND TOWERS

Fort Clonque
Alderney

For a relatively small island, Britain has experienced an extremely turbulent past, evidence of which can still be seen in the great number of fortifications spread throughout the country. Many of the most impressive medieval castles were erected as a result of internal conflict, rather than invasion. It is quite extraordinary to contemplate the time, money and resources that were ploughed into fortifying England's borders with Scotland and Wales and, in many cases, establishing protective enclaves once a territory had been invaded.

With mainland Europe so close to our shores, coastal defences have always been considered a priority. Even during times of stability, our southern counties were constantly being fortified and are still littered with a variety of structures from several centuries. Most of the largest surviving are in the care of organizations such as English Heritage, but those huge fortresses, impressive though they may be, do not represent the complete picture.

The Landmark Trust has been able to preserve and restore a number of buildings throughout Britain that reflect our military heritage, smaller forts or fragments of greater structures. It would not have been feasible to have contemplated taking on projects that were too large to sustain, even if initial repairs and renovations had been affordable. Those that the Trust has selected as suitable for transforming into guest accommodation cover a wide spectrum of period and style, although some of those occupying medieval sites are later additions.

Scottish lairds' fortified tower houses are well represented by Saddell Castle and the Castle of Park at Glenluce – solid, dour structures with little exterior charm, but whose interiors reflect an unexpectedly gracious style of living. The eighteenth and nineteenth centuries produced solidly built forts and coastal batteries intended to counter perceived threats from France. They range in size from the monumental Fort Clonque on Alderney, down to a cloverleaf-shaped, red brick Martello tower on the Suffolk coast.

Wars and conflict have sadly been a constant ingredient in British history, but they have left behind an important architectural legacy. Fortunately, the Landmark Trust has preserved some of these buildings, not merely for us to explore for a day and remember through a postcard, but to live in and experience (albeit in greater comfort) what they might have been like originally.

Castle of Park
Glenluce, Dumfries & Galloway,
Scotland

Tall and austere, the sixteenth-century
Castle of Park overlooks Glenluce village
from the brow of a nearby hill, castle and
settlement separated by the Water of Luce a
little way inland from its estuary. Although
this far south-west corner of Scotland
benefits from the benign climatic influences
of the Gulf Stream, ensuring winter snows
are rare, gale-force winds often howl
relentlessly across Luce Bay, lashing the
sparsely populated coastline with driving,
horizontal rain. On such bleak days, previous
occupants of this L-shaped tower house
must have been grateful that the main
entrance was well sheltered in the angle
created by the main body of the house and
stair tower.

Above the heavily studded door, an
inscription, now picked out in gold, states
the original owner was Thomas Hay and that
building work started in March 1590,
probably using materials from the partially
ruined twelfth-century Cistercian Abbey of
Glenluce further down the valley. Once
inside, the rather severe exterior is forgotten
as a stone staircase winds up to the living
quarters, the ground floor originally housing
a kitchen, larder, scullery and storerooms.
The first floor was taken up entirely by the
main hall, warmed by a large fireplace set
into the wall halfway along its 30-foot length

and with a small secondary staircase in one
corner providing direct servant access from
below when the household was dining.
Bedrooms and a warm, comfortable sitting
room with hand-painted decorated ceiling
have been created on the next two floors and
there is also another small room, known as a
cap house, at the top of the main stair turret.
Most rooms are considerably brighter than
they would have been originally, as
eighteenth-century refurbishment included
enlarging most of the window frames.
Recreating the castle's exact original internal
configuration has been something of an
exercise in educated guesswork, based largely
on drawings made of the castle in 1898. It
was no longer lived in after around 1830,
when all the contents and much of the wood
panelling was removed by owner James
Dalrymple-Hay to his new home.

The Castle of Park stood empty and
deteriorating until basic restoration work was
carried out midway through the twentieth
century. Initially, all floors were stripped out
and the roof replaced, to be followed some
twenty years later by a full repair of outside
walls, renewal of floors and insertion of
windows. It remained in that bare state until
the Landmark Trust began the process of
transformation from empty shell back to
historic residence.

Stogursey Castle
Stogursey, Somerset

Stogursey was one of many 'new' towns created after the Norman Conquest and was originally known as Stoke Courcy, being the estate of William de Courci, a Norman knight and steward to Henry I. It would appear from its priory and moated castle that Stogursey flourished during its early years, but declined after the Wars of the Roses. By then the castle was owned by the Percy family from Northumberland, who had no practical use for it, and so it was left gradually to decay.

The surviving part of Stogursey Castle is a curious building, possibly dating back to the seventeenth century, originally erected between the gate towers, both of which have now disappeared. Entrance can still only be gained by crossing the moat, although there is no drawbridge to haul up at night. When work began on restoring the house and castle walls, the site was apparently so overgrown that it was not even visible from the air. The whole castle enclosure is now clear, curtain walls partially repaired and repointed, the moat dredged and filled with water, and, if the 'No Fishing' signs are to be believed, restocked with fish, although one does wonder if herons can read.

Woodsford Castle
Nr Dorchester, Dorset

Those who admire the work of Thomas Hardy and delight in exploring the Dorset landscape so vividly portrayed in his novels will love Woodsford Castle. Set in the very heart of 'Hardy country' just 3 miles from Dorchester, the building has direct links with the author. His father, a builder, carried out restoration work here in 1850 and Hardy himself was a frequent visitor.

Quite a few changes have taken place since the castle was finished in 1370 for its original owner, Sir Guy de Bryan. Exposed bricks and masonry at one end indicate the building was probably larger at one stage; indeed, Woodsford was designed as a quadrangular castle with turrets and crenellations. Although three sides have crumbled into decay, the remaining part, now restored, includes the original hall, or king's rooms, the chapel and one more main room known as the queen's room. A vast thatched roof now gives the impression of a large, rambling manor house.

CONTENTS

Saddell Castle
Saddell, Strathclyde, Scotland

Immortalized in Paul McCartney's song, 'Mull of Kintyre', this long, slender peninsular retains its mainland status courtesy of a narrow isthmus occupied by the small, atmospheric fishing port of Tarbert. Saddell Bay is located halfway down the eastern side of Kintyre, and offers stunning views across Kilbrannan Sound to the rugged outline of the Isle of Arran, Scotland's most southerly island.

South from Saddell, the main centre of population is Campbeltown, a community that flourished on two typically Scottish industries, herring fishing and distilling. Although both have declined somewhat in recent years, single malt whisky from the Campbeltown area is still respected and enjoyed by aficionados.

Sheltered from prevailing easterly winds and Atlantic weather systems, Saddell is perhaps best known to visitors for the remains of a Cistercian monastery, supposedly founded in 1160 by Somerled, the first Lord of the Isles. Although he is thought to be buried here, his grave is unidentified. Nevertheless, there remains a most remarkable collection of carved grave slabs depicting animals of the hunt and heavily armed warriors. Saddell Estate itself, with castle and other cottages spread around the fringes of its bay, is well hidden from the public road down a tree-lined track, offering only pedestrian access to non-residents. With a total of twenty-three bed spaces spread between the four different Landmark Trust properties on this site (see also pp. 46–7), there could be no better or more fitting place for a large family group to constitute its own Gathering of the clan.

Saddell Castle was built in 1508 at the behest of the Bishop of Argyll in a style typical of many fortified tower houses found throughout Scotland and the Borders. Romantically sited overlooking a sandy bay at the foot of Saddell Glen, the castle was largely constructed using stone from the ruined twelfth-century monastery, located less than half a mile away.

From the beginning of the seventeenth century, the castle was owned by the Campbells, who retained their interest for most of the next four centuries. Substantial renovations were needed when it eventually came into the care of the Landmark Trust, including the removal of several well-established trees from the parapets.

The roofless walls of a cluster of stone-built outhouses still flank a cobbled courtyard approached through a stone archway. Past visitors to the castle whose motives or demeanour were deemed suspect might have thought they were about to receive traditional Highland hospitality when invited inside. However, the first step over the castle threshold might well have been their last, as floorboards immediately inside the castle entrance were removable, leaving a drop straight down into a pit dungeon. If that facility is still in operation, it could bring a whole new meaning to the hogmanay tradition of 'first footing'.

For those who do negotiate the front door safely, there is a wealth of detail to admire on the castle's different floors, such as carved stonework, painted ceilings, huge fireplaces and furnishings that perfectly match the castle's atmosphere.

Kingswear Castle
Dartmouth, Devon

In order to protect Dartmouth's harbour at the end of the fifteenth century, two castles were built facing each other near the mouth of the Dart estuary. One of these, Kingswear, is now a Landmark.

Although slightly offset to allow for effective crossfire without risk to friendly forces, the two castles were still close enough to enable a heavy chain to be suspended between them to prevent enemy shipping getting any further upriver.

The ground floor of the castle, which housed its armaments, has been left bare, exactly as it would have been when in commission; living quarters are on the floors above. A rather unusual annexe in the form of a Second World War concrete blockhouse provides additional accommodation, cleverly converted inside but still somewhat spartan in appearance.

Although a wonderful location, Kingswear Castle may not be the answer for parents of young children seeking a stress-free holiday, being built on jagged rocks that drop straight into the sea!

Dartmouth itself has fine examples of seventeenth-century architecture, but from most viewpoints the town is dominated by the red brick buildings of the Royal Naval College, set dramatically on Mount Boon overlooking the harbour and tree-lined river.

The Bath Tower
Caernarfon, Gwynedd, Wales

The Bath Tower acquired its name from having been part of a public bath house built inside Caernarfon's medieval walls in 1823, a venture designed to increase the town's appeal to visitors. In more recent times, particularly since the investiture of the Prince of Wales in 1969, Caernarfon has become one of the most popular tourist destinations in Wales, and Edward I's magnificent late thirteenth-century castle has been designated a World Heritage Site.

This powerful but elegant seven-towered fortress, whose design was inspired by the walls of ancient Constantinople, was one of many Edward built during his campaign finally to suppress Welsh opposition to English rule. It was here in 1301 that his son was installed as the first Prince of Wales, but the first royal investiture came much later in 1911 when the future Edward VIII became the new prince. Visitors will find much to explore on Anglesey: perhaps not the physical grandeur of Snowdonia, but an island richly endowed with prehistoric sites, the greatest concentration in Wales.

It would be difficult to envisage a better location than the Bath Tower from which to savour the atmosphere of such an historic place. Empty for many years before being sympathetically restored, the fortress has a first-floor living room whose two large windows offer contrasting but equally impressive views, especially at sunset. On one side, town walls and castle towers are bathed in mellow, golden light, and on the other, land and sea merge into shimmering infinity.

Morpeth Castle
Morpeth, Northumberland

Morpeth Castle has occupied the same vantage point overlooking this busy Northumbrian market town since the thirteenth century. Although most of the curtain wall is still in place, a rather splendid gatehouse is the only building that still remains; and this is now in Landmark's care. Built by William, Lord Greystoke, around 1350, the gatehouse has survived the centuries in different ownerships while the adjacent castle gradually fell into decay, its stone being used for other local buildings. Raiders from Scotland caused havoc in many northern towns and villages and the castle no doubt played its part during such skirmishes, but it was during the Civil War in 1664 that its most notable moment in history occurred. Laid siege by a Royalist force of some 2,700, the beleaguered garrison of only 500 Parliamentarian troops held out for 20 days, before marching out with honour, having sustained only 23 losses. The attacking soldiers fared less well, suffering 191 fatalities.

As the castle is not readily visible from approach roads to Morpeth town centre and has to be approached through a confusing network of residential streets, visitors arriving in the dark need to have their navigational skills honed to perfection and, even then, may still pass the entrance lane several times before reaching their goal. I speak from bitter experience and my attempts were in full daylight.

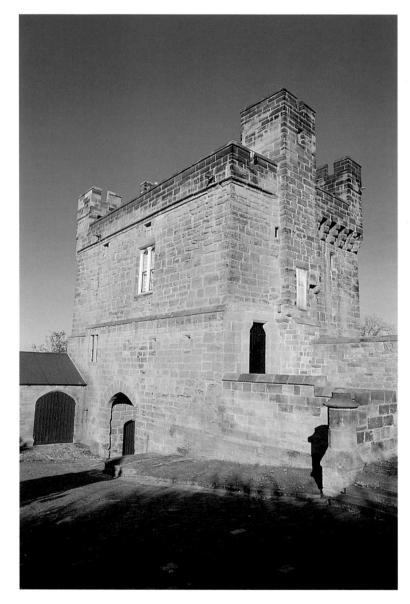

Martello Tower
Aldburgh, Suffolk

'Martello' is a generic name applied to the round brick forts that sprang up in profusion around England's south-eastern coastline at the beginning of the nineteenth century. Prior to his defeat at Waterloo in 1815, Napoleon had been preparing to launch an invasion of England and so a line of coastal defences was constructed to repel any attempted French landings. The old saying 'imitation is the sincerest form of flattery' certainly applies to Martello towers: their design was based on a similar construction that successfully repelled persistent attacks by two heavily armed British warships off the island of Corsica in 1794, an engagement fought at Mortella Point.

Erosion from centuries of relentless pounding by the North Sea has taken its toll on many coastal communities, and here the tower is the sole surviving building of Slaughden village, whose cottages have long since vanished. Even though erection of robust concrete sea-defence walls at Aldburgh has arrested the sea's progress inland, the deafening roar of storm-driven waves crashing on to the shingle beach serves as a constant reminder of nature's power.

Inside the Martello, thick walls of red brick deaden sound from outside, but the internal acoustics resulting from the domed ceiling are quite amazing. Musical instruments can sound exquisite, but one should also be aware that any indelicate whispered conversation may be considerably amplified by the time it crosses the main room.

Crownhill Fort
Plymouth, Devon

Plymouth is an integral part of British maritime history, for ever linked with great seafaring exploits. However, hidden away from the famous Hoe, Crownhill Fort dates back to the 1860s when invasion by Napoleon III was perceived as a serious threat and a ring of forts was erected around Plymouth to defend its naval base.

Crownhill was used continuously for military purposes until 1986 and acquired by the Landmark Trust a year later. Part of the officers' quarters have been converted into guest accommodation and the rest of the fort has now been restored to its original state, a mammoth undertaking given the size and scale of the fortifications. Examples of original weaponry are being added to the museum, including many larger artillery pieces for outside display.

The entire site is surrounded by a huge 30-foot dry ditch, further protected by gun emplacements and firing positions, all linked by a bewildering labyrinth of underground tunnels. Grassy banks and turf-roofed buildings create a natural disguise that would have cleverly obscured the menace within from would-be attackers

West Blockhouse
Milford Haven, Dyfed, Wales

Vertigo sufferers may not be entirely comfortable in the West Blockhouse, there being very little terra firma between the fort and rugged Pembrokeshire cliffs. Those unmoved by being perched almost directly above the crashing waves are rewarded not only by superb sea views, but also by a far greater degree of comfort than might have been supposed, given such a bleak and isolated position. Thick exterior stone walls of impeccably cut and finished limestone are internally clad with pine, providing not only good insulation but visual warmth, too, especially when the wood reflects the soft, golden light generated by the flames of an open coal fire.

Completed in 1857, armed with six heavy guns and manned by thirty-four troops, the fort was the remotest of several defensive positions commissioned to protect the entrance to Milford Haven harbour.

Approach to the Blockhouse is by a long track, running roughly parallel to a road giving access to St Ann's Head lighthouse. These two coastal outposts are separated by Mill Bay, whose sheltered aspect was the landing site chosen by Henry Tudor in 1485 when arriving to claim the English throne.

The Culloden Tower
Richmond, North Yorkshire

Built in 1746 by local MP John Yorke and named after the bloody battle that finally crushed the Stuart dynasty and established Hanoverian rule in Britain, this handsome octagonal tower stands alone in a dramatic parkland location overlooking the River Swale and historic market town of Richmond.

The Culloden Tower had been neglected for many years before being rescued and restored, but after a good deal of detective work involving the examination of photographs, drawings and surviving fragments, it has been possible to recreate much of the original internal plasterwork and carving.

The style in one room is Gothic, but perhaps the most rewarding design and craftsmanship is in the top-floor bedroom, which is of Classical origin. The ceiling is so splendid that one might feel twinges of guilt for daring to contemplate sleep.

Impressive though the Culloden Tower might be, it certainly lacks the awe-inspiring impact of its town centre counterpart, the Norman keep of Richmond Castle, which dominates the surprisingly well-preserved eleventh-century curtain walls. A somewhat less warlike structure in Richmond's architectural portfolio is the Georgian theatre. Built in 1788, it is the oldest in England and, in addition to housing a colourful museum, still stages regular performances.

Peters Tower
Lympstone, Devon

By the time the River Exe flows past the pleasant estuary village of Lympstone, it has already traversed across most of Devon from its source high up on the rolling hills of Lorna Doone's Exmoor.

The centre of Lympstone is made up of a narrow-laned jumble of Georgian and early Victorian cottages, a small railway station on the branch line linking Exeter with Exmouth (Devon's first sea-bathing resort), and a tall, colourful brick clock tower, standing right on the edge of the mud and shingle estuary bank.

Peters Tower was built in 1885 by William Peters as a memorial to his wife and remained in the same family ownership until given to the Trust on the death of William's grandson in 1979.

Odd-shaped buildings, not originally intended for human habitation, have provided Landmark Trust architects with seemingly insurmountable design problems. When one considers that the interior of Peters Tower was little more than a staircase leading up to the clock, it represents no mean feat to have incorporated living and sleeping accommodation for two into such a restricted space.

Lympstone is very much a yachting centre so there is a constant bustle of activity to observe from the tower, not least that of a sailing club almost directly below, where anxious parents gather to watch life-jacketed offspring wobble hesitantly away from shore on frequently capsizing sailboards.

Fort Clonque
Alderney, Channel Islands

Not only is Alderney the most northerly of the Channel Islands, but it is also the closest to mainland France. A coastline dotted with forts and gun emplacements bears testimony to the strategic value placed on the island's position by defenders and invaders alike.

Although many relate to German occupation during the Second World War, most of Alderney's fortifications date back to the mid nineteenth century, constructed by the British in direct response to an increase in French naval power. Fort Clonque is by far the most spectacular survivor of that era, built on a rocky outcrop linked to the shore by a causeway submerged twice a day at high tide. Consequently, close scrutiny of locally published tide tables is recommended to avoid being stranded ashore for several hours. This dramatic outpost was once manned by around fifty men with a battery of ten guns, mostly 68-pounders, none of which was ever fired in anger. Since Landmark took over the fort in 1966, the guard room, gatehouse, soldiers' quarters and a massive German gun casement have been converted into comfortable accommodation.

No matter how long the duration of one's stay, the mood of the sea is never the same two days running, and one could never tire of simply sitting on the top rampart at sunset, waiting for dusk and distant lighthouses to begin their nightly semaphore of safety to shipping.

COTTAGES

Coombe
Nr Morwerstow, Cornwall

Holiday cottages are big business, filling glossy brochures with a diverse collection of buildings ranging from barns to bungalows, all euphemistically gathered under the same architectural umbrella. It is strange how the cottage concept has such an effect on people, whether as the perfect holiday haunt or ideal retirement home, but not every country cottage has roses round the door and a log fire in the hearth. Assorted varieties of rot, no mains services and beams low enough to cause permanent brain damage all seem to act as magnets for potential owners seeking a slice of 'country' life and prepared to pay for it.

The name is derived from the medieval word 'cotage', used to describe the earliest simple peasant dwelling or shelter, often consisting of no more than turf laid over a framework of poles or branches. Timber was plentiful in the early Middle Ages and was widely used as buildings became more substantial, probably the earliest surviving examples from that period being cottages with A-shaped cruck frames. Curved tree trunks were split lengthways, the two halves then being reversed to form an arch, joined together and strengthened with a cross piece to form the A shape. The main body of the building consisted of a box frame made from timber uprights; the spaces in between were filled with wattle and daub, made by covering a lattice of hazel sticks with a mixture that might include clay, chopped straw and cow dung.

As farmers prospered, cottages became more substantial and exhibited regional variations in style and construction dependent on locally available timber or stone, thatched roofing material varying between heather, reeds or straw. It was not until the Industrial Revolution, beginning midway through the eighteenth century, that mass production led to the widespread use of brick as a basic building material, distributed by an ever-growing network of rail and canal transport. As labour was transferred from the countryside to work in newly established factories, employers built whole terraces to house their new workforce. Although not detached or out in the countryside, these were still genuine cottages, being basic accommodation for humble working folk.

Those cottages that have been restored by Landmark do not necessarily represent a definitive guide to vernacular architecture, but some certainly offer an insight into a simpler way of life carried on unchanged for generations.

Coombe
Nr Morwenstow, Cornwall

The tiny hamlet of Coombe, buried deep in
one of the narrow valleys that pierce
Cornwall's rugged Atlantic coastline, is a
perfect example of the National and
Landmark Trusts coming together to
preserve both a landscape and the buildings
contained within it. Once a working hamlet
centred around a watermill, Coombe's
cluster of cottages might have been at risk
from decay or insensitive 'improvements' if
sold off on a piecemeal basis. By purchasing
the whole estate, Landmark has ensured that
Coombe is protected as an example of a
small rural settlement.

Less than half a mile away is the wonderfully
named bay of Duckpool, which, although
little more than an indentation in the
surrounding cliffs, is one of the few places
on this stretch of coast to the north of Bude
where cars can be driven down to the sea. At
low water, a sandy beach is exposed, flanked
by lines of jagged rocks. Among the crevices
are hidden pools harbouring tiny fish, sea
anemones, elusive crabs and other shellfish,
making the beach a popular destination for
families with young children.

The southern approach to Coombe offers a
startling visual experience to first-time
visitors: most of the skyline above the valley
is filled by the huge satellite dishes and
antennae of a Ministry of Defence
communications centre. As the narrow,
twisting lane plunges steeply down through
the densely wooded valley, the symbols
of modern technology disappear from
view to be replaced by the cob and thatch
of an earlier era as the first cottages of
Coombe appear.

Mill House and Ford Cottage
Coombe, nr Morwenstow, Cornwall

Standing apart from the house, Coombe
mill probably came into existence midway
through the seventeenth century, or possibly
earlier. It was not specifically mentioned in
records until 1694 when it was identified in
a survey of the Earl of Bath's estate, of
which Coombe was then a part. The main
body of Mill House itself can be dated to
around 1700, having typically thick walls, a
huge chimney and a thatched roof.

Ford Cottage is directly across the lane from
Mill House, both properties being
immediately next to the stream that gives
the cottage its name. A calibrated depth
marker stands outside Ford Cottage,
enabling motorists to gauge the risk in
crossing the swollen stream after heavy rain.
Pedestrians exploring the hamlet keep dry
feet courtesy of a narrow footbridge.

The Tape family flourished as carpenters
and millers in Coombe during the late
nineteenth and early twentieth centuries,
diversifying into the increasing tourist trade
initially by providing refreshments for
walkers, until expanding further after the
Great War of 1914 by establishing proper
tearooms in Ford Cottage. One large room
was created by knocking down partitioning
walls, providing space for a piano, skittles
and other games, but as there was no
kitchen on the premises, food was prepared
in Mill House and carried across the lane.

The only public amenities that remain
in Coombe today are the peace and
tranquillity, there to be enjoyed at no
cost, unless, of course, one's car gets stuck
in the ford.

Margells
Branscombe, Devon

Branscombe is made up of a straggling collection of attractive stone and thatched cottages built alongside the deep coombes formed by three streams forcing their way down to the sea at Branscombe Mouth. Because of the settlement's dispersed nature, it can prove difficult to get one's bearings, but visitors to Margells need have no such qualms – the cottage stands almost directly opposite the excellent traditional pub. Although seemingly unremarkable from the outside, the interior of Margells is altogether more substantial and, indeed, poses something of a puzzle. Both the quantity and substance of the dark oak timbering used throughout suggest that the present cottage might once have formed part of a larger house, particularly as no trace of an original kitchen was found on the premises.

One first-floor room has an intriguing wall painting in one corner and all have exposed roof timbers, interspersed with white painted plaster, making them a little lighter than their ground-floor counterparts, whose low ceilings are covered with heavily moulded beams. Anyone of above-average height needs to concentrate when negotiating some of the sixteenth-century doorways in Margells, doubly so after sampling the fine Devon ales on offer across the road.

This particular section of Devon's coastline contains some of the most dramatic scenery in the county. Branscombe itself has an ancient church dating back to the eleventh century and containing a wealth of detail, including monuments to the Wadham family, founders of the Oxford college bearing their name.

Causeway House
Bardon Mill, Northumberland

Thatched roofing is perhaps more associated with southerly areas of England than the bleak countryside surrounding Hadrian's Wall. As one approaches Causeway House along a narrow, straight section of Roman road leading to the fort of Vindolanda, there is no immediate impression of thatch having been used, as both colour and outline suggest a covering of slate. Closer inspection reveals a tightly packed, thin layer of dark heather, the only surviving example of this building style in Northumberland.

The farmhouse dates back to 1770 and was inhabited until about twenty years ago, thereafter used only for storage of farm implements or animal feed. Although substantial quantities of heather were needed to make the roof sound and thoroughly weatherproof, restoration was certainly helped by it having been covered with corrugated iron sheeting, which arrested both deterioration of the thatch itself and potential rain damage to the building.

The internal layout has remained more or less unchanged from the time when accommodation for cattle and humans was under the same roof, albeit in separate rooms! A bedroom has been created in the loft directly over the old byre, enabling guests to sleep directly beneath the exposed roof timbers and knotted jumble of heather. Occasional tourist traffic heading for the Roman encampment bypasses the house via a specially created loop; school parties clutching workbooks and picnic lunches scarcely give Causeway House a second glance as they follow the path trodden by Hadrian's army almost 2,000 years ago.

Tower Hill Lodge
Llanarthney, Dyfed, Wales

This property is a simple, early nineteenth-century limewashed cottage originally built to house the caretaker of nearby Paxton's Tower, a triangular crenellated folly erected by Sir William Paxton in honour of Admiral Lord Nelson in 1811. The hill on which the tower stands is renowned as a viewpoint, providing a stunning panorama of the River Tywi valley and surrounding countryside. Views from the cottage itself are impeded by the tall hedgerows flanking a narrow lane that winds up past the lodge's small garden, but very little effort is required to saunter up Tower Hill and savour the pastoral delights of this part of Wales.

Although popular as a destination for family picnics at weekends, the tower often stands quite deserted and those who stay at the lodge can enjoy their very own folly at leisure. Paxton was the somewhat extravagant Mayor of Carmarthen, commissioning his fanciful tribute from designer Samuel Pepys Cockerell. The tower has three doors, each of which bears the same inscription to Nelson, but in a different language, namely English, Latin and Welsh.

Houghton West Lodge
New Houghton, Norfolk

When estate agents are desperate to avoid describing a property to prospective buyers as 'tiny', a favoured alternative is 'compact', implying that no time or energy will be unnecessarily wasted getting from one side of the room to another.

Houghton West Lodge would therefore qualify as an extremely compact dwelling, with sitting room, bedroom, bathroom and kitchen all clustered around a central chimney. However, any lack of space is more than made up for by its location, guarding one of the entrances to Houghton Hall, Sir Robert Walpole's magnificent Palladian mansion. He served as Britain's first prime minister from 1721 to 1742 under two monarchs, George I and George II.

A long, straight minor road, almost devoid of traffic, runs past the lodge and its large white painted gate, through silent woods towards New Houghton and the main entrance to Houghton Hall. Walpole had the original hamlet demolished in 1729 and moved to its present location as it was deemed to be spoiling the view from his residence.

Church Cottage
Llandygwydd, Dyfed, Wales

An unsignposted lane off the main Newcastle Emlyn-to-Cardigan road leads to one of those Welsh villages whose name bears only one vowel and seemingly too many consonants for non-Celtic tongues to grapple with. As a piece of architecture Church Cottage is unremarkable, but what makes it special is that this was the very first project tackled by the newly formed Landmark Trust in 1965.

The humble church-caretaker's cottage was in a very bad state when purchased by the Trust for £400 from the Church of Wales. An original room layout of two-up, two-down was augmented by basic facilities in a lean-to shed at the back of the cottage, although these did not include a bathroom, merely a kitchen sink and lavatory.

To make the property habitable once more, excavation of an earth bank to the rear created sufficient space to build on a section comprising bathroom, kitchen and a new staircase. Having replaced most of the woodwork, the cottage was then roofed with slate from Preseli, the same hills that provided the huge blue dolerite stones used by the ancient Britons to construct the mysterious circle of Stonehenge.

Pond Cottage and the Dairy
Endsleigh, nr Milton Abbot, Devon

Endsleigh is owned by a sporting syndicate and is run as a private hotel for members and their guests. They have restored much of the early landscaping, gardens and arboreta, but as some other areas of woodland were being sold off separately, the Landmark Trust was anxious to preserve some of the important buildings that once formed an integral part of the estate. Having secured the future of the Swiss Cottage (see p. 154) in 1977, attention was focused on the Dairy and Pond Cottage some six years later. These two delightful buildings stand in front of a large pond, surrounded by many different species of trees, the effect as a whole being very typical of the Picturesque movement of landscaping and architecture. In contrast to the symmetrical, regimented planting schemes of Lancelot 'Capability' Brown and others of that school, intended to form or enhance broad vistas, the Picturesque sought to create an illusion of nature untamed, most successfully achieved at Endsleigh by Humphrey Repton.

The Dairy has the necessary constant coolness that comes from the use of marble, its interior finished with intricately decorated tiles.

10, North Street
Cromford, Derbyshire

In 1771 Richard Arkwright opened the world's first water-powered cotton mill after successfully harnessing energy from the River Derwent to drive the spinning machines, an innovation that would revolutionize the textile industry. The original building still stands, but, despite being converted to house a museum, shops and other attractions, it retains a rather dark, foreboding atmosphere. Prior to this first venture into mass production, textiles had been a cottage industry, carried out by individual families scattered far and wide over the countryside. Arkwright needed several hundred workers to man his machine frames, working twelve-hour shifts in a round-the-clock operation. To house his employees, he built the world's first model village, a complete terrace of which has been preserved, including No.10, which is now the Landmark.

Windows on the first two floors are few and far between, while those on the top floors are more generous, as it was there that men would continue working at their knitting frames while their wives and children were employed at the mill.

Unlike many properties in the care of the Trust, North Street is right in the middle of an existing community. This provides guests with an opportunity to join in with life in a different environment, while giving their neighbours a new group of strangers to ponder upon each week.

St Mary's Lane
Tewkesbury, Gloucestershire

Tewkesbury has flourished since the Middle Ages, and reminders of early prosperity abound in the many impressive half-timbered buildings that still occupy prominent positions in the town centre. Many have now been converted into shops, but perhaps the most atmospheric are the old pubs, inns and hotels, several of which date back to the thirteenth and fourteenth centuries, including the Royal Hop Pole, mentioned by Charles Dickens in *The Pickwick Papers*. Tucked away behind the main thoroughfare, St Mary's Lane provides a reminder of more recent contributions to the town's economy.

During the eighteenth century, Tewkesbury became a centre for manufacturing knitted items such as stockings. These were not mass produced in mills or factories similar to those in Yorkshire and Lancashire, but made by a large number of individual home workers. The row of three tall red brick houses rescued by the Landmark Trust in 1969 exemplify where knitters lived and worked under the same roof. The rooms that contained their knitting frames are readily identified by the extra-long windows, designed to provide maximum light for an often intricate process before electricity was on hand to light premises at the flick of a switch.

Those engaged in the stocking trade must have secured a reasonable living as their tall houses are quite solidly built, although negotiating steep, narrow flights of stairs up to the top bedrooms can represent something of a challenge these days.

Frenchman's Creek
Helford, Cornwall

The crashing breakers of Cornwall's north coast seem a world away from the Helford River's gentle tidal tributaries further south on the Lizard peninsula. There are surely few more secluded hideaways than the cottage at Frenchman's Creek, secreted at the end of the narrow inlet immortalized in Daphne du Maurier's novel of the same name.

Careful navigation through a complex network of narrow lanes leads to the ultimate access point, a steep track that drops rapidly towards the creek and surrounding National Trust-owned woods. For drivers of a nervous disposition, or those without four-wheel drive during bad weather, a wheelbarrow is provided to transport luggage and supplies on the final leg.

Although very close to the creek itself, the cottage looks directly out on to a steep bank, which is covered in spring and early summer with a carpet of white-flowered wild garlic, its scent heavy on the air. At the foot of the bank, a stream rushes purposefully past the cottage's raised frontage, only to lose all impetus just a few yards further on when it is enveloped by the limpid waters of Frenchman's Creek.

The water's edge alongside the old smuggler's haunt is littered with the gaunt, skeletal outlines of fallen trees, their roots exposed by decades of erosion and no longer able to support their weight.

An occasional walker may pass by, but otherwise the silence and privacy are absolute.

Cul Na Shee
Saddell, Strathclyde, Scotland

There are probably people who would never even contemplate spending a week in a corrugated iron bungalow, but rejecting the idea out of hand is entirely missing the point of Cul Na Shee. Of course, it would be hard to find two more unfashionable ingredients, but ample rewards await those willing to set aside prejudice and preconceived ideas.

Cul Na Shee is the outermost of four Landmark properties dotted around the shoreline of Saddell Bay (see also pp. 20–21) and was originally built as a retirement home by a local teacher in the 1920s. It is totally secluded, its front porch standing just a few feet away from a foreshore of bleached pebbles that scrunch noisily underfoot and lead down to the rocky, seaweed-draped shore. Views out across the bay towards the Isle of Arran can be spectacular, especially when the granite crags of its highest peak, Goatfell, are suffused by the softening amber rays of sunset. It may sound trite to describe the cottage's pine-clad interior as 'snug and cosy', but when the curtains are drawn, the fire and lamps lit, this phrase fits very well.

Ferry Cottage
Saddell, Strathclyde, Scotland

The plain-fronted cottage faces directly out to sea, occupying the same site as its predecessor, whose footings can still be seen. The ferry that operated from Saddell was not a passenger service from one point to another, but a means of bearing goods ashore from the steamers that ploughed up and down the remoter parts of west Scotland in the days before a road network was established.

Saddell would have been just one of many similar isolated communities whose inhabitants depended on the services of a ferryman to supply them with basic necessities, including cumbersome sacks of coal and, of course, news, information and gossip from further afield. While performing an essential function for the Saddell Estate, the ferryman remained a freelance operator and owned his own boat and land. Traces of the original jetty can still be seen near the cottage and one can well imagine the noise and bustle there on days when eagerly anticipated cargo was being brought ashore. (See also pp. 20–21.)

HOUSES, HALLS AND MANORS

The White House
Aston Munslow, Shropshire

One of the great pleasures of
Ordnance Survey maps is that
they readily provide an insight
into a region's history and topo-
graphy. Within a 6-mile radius of
Aston Munslow, civilization's
progress can be traced from the
hill forts of early settlers and
Roman roads marching across a
landscape pitted with the ruined
castles of border conflict.
The White House is not named
on the map and only reveals its
true character to those who
choose to stay there. Hidden
within the whitewashed walls are
the cruck trusses of a fourteenth-
century hall, the dark wood
furnishings of Jacobean and
Tudor rooms and the remnants of
Miss Constance Purser's
Museum. This remarkable lady
set up her Museum of Buildings
and Country Life in 1966, not
only labelling parts of the
building's structure, but also
collecting agricultural and
domestic implements pertinent to
the White House and that might
provide an insight into the
simplicity of rural life as lived for
generations. It certainly was a
labour of love and visitors
benefited from her enthusiasm
and generosity for 20 years.

Of all the types of building rescued by the Landmark Trust for people to enjoy, the houses, halls and manors are some of the most important, not merely by virtue of their size or antiquity, but also because they manage to encapsulate an essential cross-section of architectural and social development from the early Middle Ages.

As with most other Landmarks, none of the houses falls into the 'showpiece' category, but yet they all remain vitally important parts of our heritage that would undoubtedly have disappeared, as there seems to be no middle ground in the preservation of certain kinds of domestic architecture. The National Trust has saved an outstanding collection of houses for the nation, but although they all merit consideration, they remain 'hands off' exhibits.

Some of the most important buildings have been restored from piles of rubble and collapsed timbers, a task requiring untold patience, research into archive material and a collection of dedicated and highly skilled conservation architects and builders, able to interpret and recreate the construction methods and materials so successfully used by their medieval counterparts. One of the most important and versatile ingredients was lime and, although scarcely employed since the nineteenth century, this now forms an integral part of any renovations, being used for cement, plaster and paint. Its extraordinary characteristics of porosity and flexibility allow ancient timber-frame structures to move and breathe, vital functions not possible with modern equivalents.

In addition to saving important medieval structures, Landmark has also acknowledged the work of two important architects from more recent times: Edwin Lutyens and Charles Rennie Mackintosh, who have both made significant and stylish contributions to our architectural history.

The Landmark 'experience' is available to everybody and can be approached in a variety of ways. Some visitors may include a television in their luggage, treating a medieval manor house as a thatched theme-park break; others want to come closer to the original atmosphere. It is quite amazing to discover the difference between electric and candle light in a cavernous timbered hall – roof beams suddenly become so high that feeble flames scarcely have the power to illuminate them, producing a vague impression of dark shapes, but nothing more. Even those who do bring the 'box' with them should leave it off for one night, just to be part of the magic.

Sackville House
East Grinstead, West Sussex

Sackville House is one of several fine, half-timbered, medieval buildings that still grace part of East Grinstead's High Street. At the other end of town, a later period of development centred around the railway, the advent of which rapidly increased the town's prosperity. Consequently, architectural age differences are clearly defined and it is refreshing to see Sackville House and neighbouring buildings having room to breathe, rather than fighting for space in an avalanche of advancing red brick.

Originally built around 1520 during the reign of Henry VIII, the internal layout has changed little over the years, but even more remarkable is that the 600-foot long garden has survived intact. Surrounding houses of the same period had similar narrow plots of land, referred to as portlands, running behind them, but many have now been divided or developed. The last owner of Sackville House bequeathed it to the Landmark Trust, thereby ensuring long-term security for both house and garden.

East Grinstead is a perfect base from which to visit some of the architectural treasures located nearby. Knole, seat of the Sackville family and birthplace of Vita Sackville-West, Batemans, home of Rudyard Kipling, and Winston Churchill's Chartwell are just a few. There is, however, one drawback to any ambitious sightseeing programme. Once the High Street door has been closed, stunning views from the gardens across to remnants of primeval forest, combined with Sackville's extremely agreeable atmosphere, deter many would-be tourists from venturing out at all.

Peake's House
Colchester, Essex

Colchester is England's oldest town, founded by the Romans on the site of an even earlier settlement after their invasion of the south-east in AD 43. Centuries later, it was the Normans who left their mark on the town by building a huge castle, whose keep is the largest surviving example in Europe.

In the latter part of the sixteenth century, refugee Flemish weavers colonized the district of Colchester where Peake's House stands, an area still referred to as the Dutch Quarter. Sadly, there is no particular historic or romantic attachment to the benefactor's name, Mr Peake being a local property owner who passed it on to the local council in 1946. Restricted vehicular access has ensured that narrow lanes surrounding the Landmark retain much of their original atmosphere.

Cottages dating back to the fourteenth and sixteenth centuries have been amalgamated at some point to form the present house, both sections of which still have the large mullioned windows used to provide maximum daylight for the weavers. The thriving wool trade during that period created great wealth, a prosperity reflected in some of the region's magnificent 'wool' churches.

Purton Green
Stansfield, Suffolk

If the Landmark Trust had not been able to purchase the crumbling remains of Purton Green in 1969, the property would by now almost certainly have disintegrated beyond repair into nothing more than a forlorn heap of rotting timbers. Thanks to the Trust's timely intervention, this important timber-framed hall-house dating back to about 1250 has been saved, one of no more than half a dozen similar examples still existing in the country.

Situated on the course of what was once a road from Bury St Edmunds, Purton Green is a surviving fragment from one of England's hundreds of lost villages. Following the Black Death, which virtually halved Britain's population midway through the fourteenth century, many villages were either abandoned or cleared to make sheep walks by landowners unable to secure sufficient labour for arable farming from decimated communities.

Because of its ruinous state, the repair of Purton Green necessitated the use of far more new materials than the Trust would have liked, as there was little opportunity to blend old and new seamlessly as with other restorations. One of the benefits

of this approach, however, is that visitors can clearly identify those segments of the old hall that have required totally new wood, leading to a greater understanding of the complexity of such an undertaking and an appreciation of the skills of those dedicated craftsmen who secured the building's future.

The hall section has been restored to its original state by the removal of a medieval floor and chimney stack, but no attempt has been made to incorporate it into the living accommodation. Modern facilities have been created in the high end of the building, which was probably added on to the house around 1600, leaving the hall part to be enjoyed for what it is, rather than as a 'designer' living room with scissor-braced trusses.

As befits a lost village, Purton Green is indeed hidden away in undulating farmland and can only be approached on foot; a substantial wheelbarrow is available to help with the final quarter of a mile along a grassy footpath.

Any guests tempted to curse as they trundle through the rain might spare a thought for the housekeeper, who makes the same journey several times on changeover days.

Wortham Manor
Lifton, Devon

If there is one place above all others where one can be 'Lord of the Manor', it must surely be at Wortham. The house that exists today is an early sixteenth-century remodelling of an existing medieval house, and from 1501 it was the chief seat of the Dinham family. Thankfully, the building was also sensitively restored in 1945 and has not been spoilt by drastic alterations over the years. When renovation and repairs were undertaken by the Trust in 1969, however, the whole structure needed completely re-roofing, a process that did at least provide an opportunity for discovering Wortham's original layout. The house is L-shaped with a long east wing to the rear, and has its own ample grounds enhanced by a delightful setting that has been preserved through the Trust buying up adjacent farm buildings.

Although the building as an entity is impressive, what gives Wortham Manor that particularly memorable feel are the interior and exterior details. The main doorway is surrounded by an elaborately carved entrance portal of dressed granite, almost identical to the style that adorns the College at nearby Week St Mary (see p. 102).

The similarity is due to the involvement of John Dinham in both projects, Wortham being his own residence while the College, where he supervised the sixteenth-century school's construction, was built by his cousin, Thomasine Bonaventure. Granite has also been used to good effect to surround the many lead-latticed windows, through which sunlight beams diamond patterns on to floors and walls. It is the quality of timberwork through the house that really impresses. Previously concealed above a ceiling, the chamber roof has now been exposed, exhibiting a wealth of moulded timbers and arch braces, while directly below in the hall itself, a mass of dark, heavily carved oak adds to the almost perfectly preserved Jacobean atmosphere. Long benches run either side of the dining table, which has solid, tapestry-backed chairs at either end for whoever are elected lord and lady of the manor. Sitting rooms have more modern, comfortable seating in which to relax and there are beds for up to fifteen guests, making Wortham Manor the ultimate venue for an extra-special family celebration.

The Old Place of Monreith
Port William, Dumfries & Galloway, Scotland

The Whithorn peninsular is steeped in religious history and many of its sites are associated with early Christianity, notably Whithorn Priory, which stands on the site of a monastery church founded by St Ninian in the fourth century.

Known locally as Dowies, the Old Place of Monreith was once home of the Maxwell family, whose descendants include author Gavin, who wrote his best-selling book about otters, *Ring of Bright Water*, in a cottage much further north, overlooking the Isle of Skye.

Despite being only 2 miles from the coast, the Old Place has a landlocked bleakness, and a collection of farm buildings in the distance is its only neighbour. Approach to the Landmark is by a long, often muddy gated track requiring appropriate footwear to avoid sinking ankle-deep in one's best shoes.

The house had been empty for twenty years prior to restoration and was without roof and floors, but at least the fireplaces were still intact. During alterations, the original turnpike staircase was reinstated, giving access to bedrooms on both first and attic floors. This allows up to eight people to sample life in a lowland laird's house in a remote, seldom-visited but ultimately rewarding part of Scotland.

Ascog

Isle of Bute, Strathclyde, Scotland

The Isle of Bute has been a favourite holiday destination with Glaswegians since the nineteenth century, as it is easily reached from the Clyde coast by a regular ferry service from Wemyss Bay, a small port boasting a superb wrought iron and glass railway station. Rampant Victoriana continues in Rothesay, Bute's only town, where further displays of municipal ironwork await disembarking passengers. These include the seafront's star attraction, the 'Victorian Conveniences', whose style and comfort have to be experienced and put their modern-day counterparts to shame. Definitely value for money, although slightly more expensive than a 'penny'.
A few miles down the sheltered east coast is the Ascog Estate, where two Landmark properties (see also pp. 60–61) share extensive wooded grounds approached by a long entrance drive of mature beech trees. Ascog House is the older of the two houses, having been built by John Stewart in 1678. He probably enlarged an even older structure, as some features in the house relate to earlier building practices, notably the stair tower and cap house. With crow-stepped gables and steep roof, it now looks like the typical laird's

house it was intended to be, although it took a huge amount of work to get it back to something like its original form. Some time during the nineteenth century, the house almost doubled in size following the addition of servants' quarters to the rear, a drawing room and staircase to the right of the front door. To make these alterations, ground levels had been changed, exposing foundations that could eventually have resulted in structural insecurity.
When Landmark addressed the problem in 1989, it was decided that most of the later work had to be demolished and the earth put back to original levels. The staircase was retained, but in a separate tower that now houses an en suite bedroom set apart from the main house, perhaps an ideal place to accommodate unruly and noisy children.
The restoration was almost complete when fire broke out and virtually gutted the whole building; repairs took almost two more years. Consequently, almost everything contained within Ascog House is new, apart from certain stonework that survived the blaze, but the work has been accomplished so skilfully that the interior retains its original atmosphere.

Meikle Ascog
Isle of Bute, Strathclyde, Scotland

Robert Thom purchased Ascog House and the 420-acre estate in 1831, building Meikle Ascog nine years later. Thom was a highly respected and successful engineer whose reputation had been enhanced considerably just four years before he moved to Ascog by his design of a system to provide water to Greenock on the Firth of Clyde.

Thom's association with Bute had begun some years earlier when he was buying up the Rothesay cotton mills, then powered by water from Loch Fad, a supply that subsequently proved inadequate to drive the machines. The business went bankrupt after a period of importing coal as an alternative power source, but was revitalized later when Thom devised a new method of harnessing power from the loch, much to the chagrin of Lord Bute, whose own supplies were affected.

Meikle Ascog appears to have been designed using the same logical approach employed by Thom in his work, an efficient layout ensuring that each room derived maximum benefit from light and view. Extra-low sills in the dining and drawing rooms provided occupants with uninterrupted views out to sea, even when seated.

Thom allowed further development of the estate, but ensured it was strictly controlled, barring any building on the coastal fringe. His far-sighted policy has ensured that most of the houses, including Ascog (see pp. 58-9) and Meikle Ascog, remain concealed from view, scattered around the heavily wooded hillside, thus leaving the impression of an undisturbed landscape.

Field House
Minchinhampton, Gloucestershire

Field House is constructed from irregular-sized blocks of mellow Cotswold limestone. This most commonly used building material in surrounding towns and villages endows each with its own distinctive colour variations, depending on where the stone was quarried.

The house, which has existed in its current form since around 1884, was originally four separate dwellings grouped round a small courtyard. This was subsequently roofed over and the area incorporated into what became a large farmhouse. As no major structural alterations have been carried out to 'modernize' Field House, its internal configuration remains exactly as it was when a collection of one-up, one-down cottages. The rooms may be small, but they are wonderfully lit by larger-than-expected windows, allowing one perhaps to indulge in a version of the Mad Hatter's tea party, clutching a favourite book and moving from chair to chair round the house as the sun lights different rooms in turn.

Nearby Minchinhampton Common is a vast upland area of limestone turf, providing a perfect habitat for many species of wild flower, and some of the best walking in the Cotswolds.

Gurney Manor
Cannington, Somerset

Bringing Gurney Manor back to life in its original medieval form took eight years of painstaking work, rewarding the intuition of those whose initial diagnosis had been that something special existed beneath many later additions. Fortunately, no attempts at structural modernization had been made during conversion into flats; what existed had simply been covered over, making its eventual restoration easier to manage. Solving the architectural puzzle took nine months with one discovery leading to another until an almost complete picture of the manor's past had been assembled, a history that began in the fourteenth century with its first owners whose name the house retains, the Gurney family. Landmark has endeavoured to return the house to its original room arrangement, slotting in necessary additions such as bathrooms in places that would not interrupt the layout. Every attempt has been made to emulate the high standards used to build Gurney Manor – walls have been finished with traditional lime plaster and any new timber beams needed to replace worn roof trusses were hand-adzed exactly as they would have been originally.

Plas Uchaf
Nr Corwen, Clwyd, Wales

The Berwyn Mountains cannot compete with Snowdonia in terms of height or dramatic scenery, but they do contain the highest waterfall in Wales, the 240-foot drop of Pistyll Rhaeadr, and help form an attractive backdrop to Plas Uchaf and the Dee Valley. This area also figures prominently in Welsh history, as fifteenth-century hero Owen Glendower assumed the name from one of his estates near Corwen, just a few miles down-river. Glendower led what started as a local dispute but somehow escalated into a full-scale national uprising, causing considerable problems for Henry IV.

Plas Uchaf is one of those buildings whose exterior gives no indication whatsoever of the architectural drama that lies within. Set back slightly from the road on a sharp bend, it can almost pass unnoticed as no particular features catch the eye, but closer inspection reveals a front door and windows of some antiquity. Entry is normally by a rear door, opening into a kitchen and adjacent small, comfortable sitting room. The rest of the building's length is taken up by a timbered medieval hall that is simply breathtaking in its size and beauty.

This rare Welsh example of a hall-house was probably built around 1400, but was almost derelict when drawn to the attention of the Landmark Trust. Subsequent inspection of the ruins suggested that restoration was possible, largely owing to the soundness of the massive oak roof timbers, toughened and cured by centuries of smoke from open fires.

The craftsmanship exhibited in the roof's construction is quite exceptional, although its height makes it frustratingly difficult to inspect at close quarters. The geometry of roof trusses and braces is extremely complex, each having its own vital role in supporting the structure as a whole. The other notable feature in the hall is a massive fireplace at one end. Its successful lighting and management is something of an art and can occupy far more time than might be imagined in an age where heating usually comes from the flick of a switch.

The hall has been simply furnished and it is no surprise to discover that Plas Uchaf is one of the most popular choices for Christmas holidays. A long table runs down the centre and, with comfortable armchairs parked either side of the hearth, celebrations could not be held in a more convivial atmosphere.

Calverley Old Hall
N. Leeds, West Yorkshire

Suburbs of the West Yorkshire towns of Leeds and Bradford are now virtually united in one vast urban sprawl, on the northern fringes of which is Calverley Old Hall. Not even the very best pair of rose-tinted spectacles could transform Calverley into a pastoral idyll and gentle picnic expeditions are unlikely, but to overlook Calverley Old Hall simply because of its setting would be unfair. The rambling stone buildings may be unattractively blackened by years of industrial grime, but they encompass a history dating back to the thirteenth century. Not only is there architectural evidence to piece together the Old Hall's growth over the intervening years, but records and papers have also been meticulously preserved from an early date, showing clearly how the Calverley family developed over generations. The range of buildings that makes up the Old Hall was bought by the Trust in 1979 when offered for sale in three lots, having spent almost 250 years divided up as individual cottages. Because almost no alterations had been made during that time, the house as it originally existed had, in effect, remained intact and was deemed worthy of saving.

To complete the entire project will be a long, painstaking and expensive task, but considerable progress has been made and the north wing has been converted to form the Landmark. That portion of the Old Hall, added during the first half of the seventeenth century by Sir Henry Calverley, represented the last major addition and contained a splendid dining room that now forms the current, heavily beamed living room. This

conversion took a great deal of work, as the wing comprised two partly burnt cottages before restoration began.

Sir Henry was the survivor of a family tragedy that probably would have enthralled modern-day tabloid editors (and their readers). It would appear that Henry's father, Walter, went berserk one day in 1605 and murdered two of his three sons, before later dying himself under torture. The Landmark Trust reassures guests that the foul deed was not perpetrated in any of the rooms they stay in, so there is no chance of sleep being disturbed by ghostly apparitions. The oldest parts of the building are found in the solar wing, the medieval equivalent of a sun lounge. Originally timber framed, it was remodelled and enlarged around 1400 using stone instead of wood in the construction. The great hall itself originated in about 1480 and has a carved hammerbeam roof to support its 30-foot span. An indication of the room's volume can be gauged by the fact that a fireplace occupying the north wall was converted to form two separate rooms.

A reduced version of the great hall's roof can be found in the chapel, as both were erected around the same time. The chapel is an extremely rare example of its kind, with an upper gallery for the family who had private access from the solar wing.

The solar and hall have been stripped down to bare shells in preparation for restoration at a later date, but they can still be studied and enjoyed by all who stay in the Old Hall.

Shelwick Court
Nr Hereford, Herefordshire

As with several other Landmarks, first impressions of Shelwick Court are misleading as the exterior view does not reveal the building's true character. Appearing at the end of a gently sloping drive to be a neat, gleaming stone house with central door surrounded by symmetrical windows, roofed with bright clay tiles, Shelwick Court could almost have been cut out from the pages of a child's picture book. Such comparisons are quickly forgotten, however, upon seeing the wealth of huge medieval timbers exposed internally during restoration. Even more remarkable is the fact that Shelwick Court was close to being lost for ever.

The last owner had moved into an adjacent caravan because of the building's instability. After his death, a routine inspection by a local council conservation officer prior to the building's almost certain demolition, led to it being bought and saved by the Landmark Trust. As the stone front had been dated to around 1700, the assumption was that the rest of the building might have been of roughly the same age. However, in places where plaster had fallen off walls, timber framing had been exposed. This encouraged the officer to explore further up into the attic, at some personal risk, where he discovered a superb medieval roof of six bays, crossed and supported by enormous chamfered beams.

Architectural detective work has revealed

that part of the house goes back to around 1400 and was originally the cross wing of a great hall in an even larger house. Perhaps even more surprising was the discovery that the entire medieval section had previously been dismantled and reassembled, probably when the later alterations were made, but it was impossible to determine whether this was the original site.

Every effort has been made during restoration to limit the use of new, visually obtrusive timber, so, although some vital sections had to be replaced, others were saved using hidden steel plates. Panels of original wattle and daub found in the wall frames have been augmented with new material, made in the traditional method, even down to the addition of cow dung. Walls throughout the house have been coated with lime-hair plaster and painted with limewash. Glass salvaged from nineteenth-century greenhouses has been fitted to new windows, and reclaimed stone and tiles cover the floor so that, although some sections of the building have had to be comprehensively renovated, the blend between new and original is almost seamless. No documentation or records have been found to identify the original owners of Shelwick Court, a mystery that somehow heightens the pleasure derived from staying in this anonymous medieval masterpiece.

Elton House
Bath, North-East Somerset

Abbey Green is a small, intimate square but, sadly, one of several locations in Bath affected by a Victorian penchant for tree-planting in public places. During summer months, dense foliage from the huge plane tree almost fills the square, somewhat diminishing its visual appeal. But it does at least provide welcome shade for visitors exploring Bath on foot; somewhere to rest, perhaps, while sampling the famous Bath buns sold from Sally Lunn's House, originally a seventeenth-century cake shop, just round the corner from Abbey Green. Fortunately, Elton House is just out of reach of the tree, allowing ample daylight to flood in through all sixteen windows facing on to the square. The building and most of its contents were donated to the Trust by its last owner, Miss Philippa Savery, whose initial involvement with the property began in 1946, when she rented part of an existing ground floor cobbler's shop from which to sell antiques. Upper floors at that time were let as apartments and, as tenants moved out, Miss Savery took over their leases, eventually buying the freehold when the owner died in 1962. Those who stay in Elton House will find that endearing hotchpotch of furniture and decoration often associated with antique dealers' houses – unrelated items from different periods that were kept from sale and retained, not always matching but somehow successfully blending together.

Marshal Wade's House
Bath, North-East Somerset

Wade will always be associated with the campaign to subdue rebellious Scottish clans after the failed Jacobite rebellion in 1715, as it was he who established a network of military roads to provide the English army with easier access to the very heart of the Highlands. Promoted to field marshal in 1744, his link with Bath resulted from serving as its Member of Parliament.
The elegant pale stone of Wade's former residence has been meticulously restored and cleaned, the interior detail and furnishings recreated and chosen with equal care.
As the house directly overlooks the square containing some of Bath's main tourist attractions (the Roman Baths, Pump Room and magnificent abbey), it can occasionally be rather noisy outside – often entertaining, but certainly never dull or particularly annoying.
As daylight fades, visitors and buskers drift away and the abbey precincts again fall silent, leaving those staying in Marshal Wade's House to savour the atmosphere of this wonderful setting. If there is an English equivalent of E. M. Forster's Florentine 'room with a view', this surely must be it. The abbey's gloriously decorated west front is so close that it almost seems possible to reach out and touch the carved angels clambering up towards heaven on golden limestone ladders.

The Music Room
Lancaster, Lancashire

Walking towards the Music Room on Sun Street, through Lancaster's modern, bustling town centre, it is hard to imagine a time when gardens might have existed in what is now a mass of stone and concrete. Yet that was indeed the case in the eighteenth century when the building that is now a Landmark was a garden pavilion, a fact borne out by a map dated 1778 that shows it overlooking a formally laid-out garden. Similar buildings were quite common around 1700, used by owners to survey areas of garden that perhaps they were unable to appreciate from ground level. This was in direct contrast to later pavilions, which were intended to be an integral part of a wider landscape, a design feature more than a practical structure.

Although named the Music Room and equipped with a piano, this building could, in fact, be called the Muses, as amply illustrated by the plasterwork round the walls of the Landmark's feature room. Busts of the nine Muses with symbols of their art adorn the walls in graphic relief, while the ceiling is covered by an equally exuberant collection of emperors, intermingled with other motifs of birds and flowers. This superb plasterwork was probably created by Italian craftsmen, who were known to have

worked on other houses at that time, several in Lancashire itself.

The Landmark Trust's attempt to rescue the Music Room was anything but straightforward. Although the pavilion had been known to be in distress for some time, no serious remedial action had been taken by any other organizations or local authority. Initially, the main problem was to purchase and remove the four other buildings completely surrounding it before work could even begin.

Repairs to the external fabric secured the structure of the building, but the major difficulty was renovating the plasterwork, most of which had fallen from the walls and ceiling, a process accelerated by a leaking roof. Restoration of the plasterwork took 6,000 man-hours to complete, and existing sections were reused where possible or the original work imitated with new material where necessary.

A flat has been created in the attic, leaving the Music Room empty to be enjoyed to the full. The acoustics are marvellous and, when lights are dimmed, shadows bring the sculptures alive in appreciation of the music. Whether it be 'Music' or 'Muses' seems somehow irrelevant; all that really matters is that it has been saved.

The Wardrobe
Salisbury, Wiltshire

Holiday postcards bearing the message 'Having a wonderful time in the Wardrobe' may well cause raised eyebrows, and, although this may not be the most spacious of Landmarks, a position in Salisbury's cathedral close certainly qualifies it as having one of the finest views in England. The name relates, in fact, to a period when the building was used as the bishop's storehouse, but it was converted for domestic use around 1600.

Most of the splendid rooms created at that time now house the museum of the Berkshire and Wiltshire Regiment, but extensive and costly repairs to the long-empty property were needed prior to the museum's relocation. In return for its help with the project, the Landmark Trust was allowed to create its own flat in the Wardrobe's attic, the sitting-room windows of which look directly across to Salisbury Cathedral, crowned by its slender 400-foot spire. The view is quite magnificent and changes constantly with the light, each subtle nuance picking out some new detail on the fabric. Perhaps the most remarkable thing about the cathedral is that it was designed and built as a single entity in only thirty-eight years. Conceived in 1220 by Bishop Richard Poore, it represents a stunning example of early English architecture, the first phase of the Gothic, when all was simple, harmonious and light after the gloom of the great Norman churches.

7 St Michael's Street
Oxford, Oxfordshire

Increased traffic congestion in recent years has meant that visitors to Oxford are discouraged from using their cars in the city. Those who do insist on driving are likely to spend more time inside their vehicles than exploring the numerous historic university colleges, most of which are tucked away behind the main thoroughfares.

One such hideaway is the Oxford Union Building in St Michael's Street, where the Landmark Trust has an apartment occupying a floor and a half in what was once the official residence of the debating society's steward. This part of the elegant Edwardian building was made available after the Trust contributed to the repair and restoration of the Union's original debating chamber, built in 1856 and now used as the library. Perhaps the most notable decorative features of the chamber that the Union was anxious to preserve are the hand-painted ceiling and window bays, completed during the summer vacation by a group of young artists that included Edward Burne-Jones and William Morris.

Being located in the midst of university life means that St Michael's Street is not likely to be an entirely peaceful retreat, but there could be no better location from which to savour the very essence of Oxford college life.

Goddards
Abinger Common, Surrey

The narrow lane to Abinger Common is flanked by dense trees whose gnarled and twisted roots protrude menacingly from high sandy banks on either side. It is almost a relief to emerge back into full daylight alongside a triangular green with village stocks and public whipping post still intact. Evidence of rather more genteel times is represented by the tall chimneys of Goddards, designed by Edwin Lutyens in traditional Surrey style for businessman Frederick Mirrielees in 1898.

This remarkable early example of the architect's work was not conceived as a private dwelling; its intended use was described in 1913 by a writer on Lutyens as being 'a Home of Rest to which ladies of small means might repair for holiday'. A tranquil courtyard garden sandwiched between the house's two wings offered a place for relaxation, while, in direct contrast, an indoor skittle alley probably brought a little excitement and laughter into drab lives.

Sadly, the businessman's altruism was fairly short-lived, as the house was converted for domestic use by his son in 1910, thereafter remaining in private ownership until donated to the Lutyens Society in 1991.

The Mackintosh Building
Comrie, Tayside, Scotland

Aladdin's Cave could surely not have offered up a greater array of goods than those squeezed on to the shelves and counters of Brough and Macpherson, a traditional draper and ironmonger's shop in the heart of Comrie, a small resort town on the River Earn to the west of Perth. On any one day, the window display could include items ranging from shiny galvanized dustbins, garden implements and stepladders, through to saucepans, kettles, china teapots, glassware and assorted trinkets, all fighting for space with sheepskin mittens, woolly hats and scarves. Inside the shop are drawers full of ribbons and thread and trays full of buttons to suit every conceivable size and colour of garment.

The building, which houses this nostalgic reminder of how shops used to be before supermarkets full of blister-packs and checkout counters arrived, was designed by renowned Scottish architect Charles Rennie Mackintosh in 1903. The Landmark is the flat situated directly over the shop and has a curious turret protruding out over the main street, offering a perfect vantage point from which to watch life go by, albeit at a very leisurely pace.

LUNDY

Bay of Lundy

Lundy Island is the three-mile-long summit of an undersea mountain rising to over 400 feet above the Bristol Channel. Although frequently battered by Atlantic storms, Lundy benefits from the warming influence of Gulf Stream currents, enabling its crystal-clear waters to support a rich diversity of marine life that includes rare species of coral. As a result, it was designated Britain's first Marine Nature Reserve in 1986.

The National Trust purchased the island in 1969, thereafter leasing it to the Landmark Trust, which spent twenty years repairing dilapidated buildings and installing essential services to cater for the many visitors from the mainland coming either on day trips or to stay in one of the twenty-three different properties available to rent.

The island's name originates from the old Norse word for puffin – 'lunde' – and its rugged western coastline of granite cliffs and hidden coves is full of seabird colonies, which create a cacophony of sound during the breeding season.

The island's settlement is located towards the south-eastern tip, above a small curved bay offering the only safe landing site, and it is here that Lundy's own ship, the MS *Oldenburg*, delivers passengers and supplies, transferred ashore by motor launch.

Lundy has been home to some fairly villainous characters. The Marisco family was one of the first to achieve notoriety, using the island as a lair from which to launch raids on the mainland, towards the end of the twelfth century.

A succession of largely absentee owners followed, until stability and a degree of prosperity finally began in 1834 when William Heaven became the new owner, succeeded as Squire of Lundy in 1883 by his son the Rev. Hudson Heaven, who was responsible for building the large Victorian church of St Helena. It comes as no surprise to discover that during the eighty years of that family's ownership, the island became known as the 'Kingdom of Heaven'.

The absence of cars and man-made noise endows Lundy with a tranquillity that once savoured is difficult to ignore, and guests return year after year to absorb the island's magic. Although Lundy can no longer be referred to as the 'Kingdom of Heaven', there are many who would say it is very close to paradise.

Castle and Keep Cottages

Lundy's castle was built by Henry III in 1244, after the Sheriff of Devon decreed that the island should never again be allowed to fall into such a lawless state as during the turbulent era of the piratical Marisco family. Construction costs were supposedly met from the sale of rabbits, as the island was at that time a royal warren (one hardly dare contemplate how many might have been needed to finance such a project).

During the reign of Edward III in the fourteenth century, the island was given to the Earl of Salisbury and his heirs. Ownership thereafter changed through inheritance or marriage for a further 400 years, apart from periods of confiscation during the Wars of the Roses and the Commonwealth.

A recent archaeological survey found evidence suggesting that there had been a furnace next to the castle. This supported the theory that a previous governor of Lundy, Sir Thomas Bushell, operated a mint during the Civil War to supply silver coins for Charles I's ill-fated campaign. The island held out for the royalist cause long after capitulation on the mainland.

It could be argued that the restored castle's visual appeal has been somewhat diminished by the retention of Lundy's old post office and telegraph cable station, once housed in the sloping roofed addition to its northern wall. However, it was decided that as the building provided such spectacular views along the coastline and had played an essential role in island communication with

the outside world, it was worth saving as a holiday retreat.

From 1909 until 1926, postmaster Frederick Allday conducted weekly postal deliveries every Thursday (weather permitting) with his donkey, Irwin. As the mail boat usually hove-to for a couple of hours, islanders had the opportunity of responding quickly to incoming mail, although it must have been a constant frustration for those living furthest from the castle.

Records show that the castle had decayed and been rebuilt several times since the thirteenth century. The central keep took its current form of three cottages when repaired by William Heaven during the 1850s to house his labourers, men with wonderfully resonant West Country names, including Withycombe the herdsman, Sam Jarman, a mason, and carpenter Joseph Dark.

By the time the Landmark Trust took over the island in 1969, the buildings were once more in a ruinous state, having been abandoned as dwellings some forty years earlier. In an elevated location overlooking the landing bay and consequently exposed to the harshest weather, the castle had suffered serious erosion over the years and needed a great deal of remedial work to arrest the decline. Badly crumbled mortar and collapsed sections of masonry meant that securing the outside walls alone took three summers to complete. Corrugated iron has been used to create new roofs as slates would probably be torn off by the force of Atlantic winter gales.

Millcombe House

Originally known as the Villa, Millcombe House was built in classical style for William Heaven shortly after he bought Lundy Island in 1834. A man of considerable wealth who had benefited from his godfather's successful Jamaican sugar plantations, Heaven had secured the island as a summer retreat and the villa was to be the family's residence.

Occupying a sheltered wooded valley between the village and landing bay, the house was built of stuccoed granite and designed with an inward sloping roof to catch precious rainwater. Construction must have been a logistical nightmare, as most of the materials had to be shipped over from the mainland and laboriously dragged up to the site by sled. Following the death of Mrs Heaven in 1851, the family took up permanent residence on the island, and William's son and successor the Rev. Hudson Heaven joined them in 1863. The Millcombe House of today has been completely refurbished and restored to its original appearance, decorated with appropriate nineteenth-century furniture and paintings, enabling those who stay there to wind back the clock and savour the Victorian elegance and comfort enjoyed by the Heaven family.

Admiralty Lookout

This isolated outpost was always known as
Tibbetts until it was rechristened in 1992
with a name reflecting its original function as
a signal and watch station built by the
Admiralty in 1906.

Tibbetts was the first island property to be
converted for use as a holiday cottage
following Martin Harman's purchase of
Lundy in 1925, and, although repaired and
renovated by the Landmark Trust, its
distance from the village has precluded the
installation of mains services. Consequently,
anyone staying in the Lookout will
experience life without electricity, bath,
shower or inside lavatory and water has
to be hand pumped. Despite the absence
of amenities taken for granted in modern
society, Admiralty Lookout remains a
popular choice for those seeking the
true island experience, happy to eschew
home comforts.

Perhaps a little eccentricity is a prerequisite
for deriving maximum enjoyment from this
property, a characteristic one could certainly
ascribe to Mrs Smith-Saville who stayed
during the 1930s. It would appear that she
delighted in not only entertaining the island
agent's wife to tea from a silver service, but
also thought nothing of paddling her canoe
round to the village instead of walking the
one and three-quarter miles across land.
Admiralty Lookout is surrounded by a
recently built retaining stone wall, designed
to keep the island's stock away from the
building. This at least guarantees no
unpleasant surprises during any night-time
excursions to the lavatory.

The Old Light

Modern navigational aids have substantially
reduced the risk of accidents at sea, but until
the Old Light's beam first pierced the
night sky in 1820, Lundy had posed a
very real threat to shipping. Indeed,
construction of the lighthouse was funded
by Bristol merchants anxious to safeguard
their investments.

This was Britain's highest lighthouse, with a
beam visible for 32 miles, but although the
concept of locating a beacon as high as
possible to ensure maximum visibility is
generally sound, the theory turned out to be
flawed in this case. Those responsible had
not considered the dense fog and low cloud
that frequently swirl around the island's
plateau, rendering visual warnings quite
useless at times. This problem ultimately
proved insurmountable and so the light was
eventually replaced by low-level alternatives
at either end of the island.

The lighthouse was classed as a shore station,
enabling keepers to live on the island with
their families, thereby substantially boosting
the island's resident population. The quarters
that are now Landmark flats housed two
separate families, who were able to maintain
a degree of self-sufficiency by keeping pigs
and growing vegetables.

Landmark has repaired the lantern gallery
with African hardwood and replaced the
glass. Although it is something of a stiff
climb up the spiral staircase, one's efforts
are rewarded by stunning views in every
direction, making it easy to understand
why Beacon Hill was initially chosen for
the lighthouse.

Hanmers

Hanmers occupies a prominent position overlooking Lundy's east coast, facing directly towards the distant grey smudge of Devon. As the small weatherboarded cottage sleeps four, children holidaying with their parents might fervently hope that theirs do not instigate a daily routine similar to one employed in the 1940s by the lady after whom the house was named. Mrs Hanmer's offspring started each day with a swim in the ocean, were given breakfast and then packed off for the day with meagre rations of bread and chocolate, return not being permitted until supper time at 6 p.m. A good night's sleep might have depended on how well the children prepared their own beds, as mattresses were made from freshly cut bracken. After many years visiting Lundy as a fisherman, George Thomas settled here with his family around the end of the nineteenth century, building a timber and corrugated iron cottage known as the Palace on this site. When the Thomases left Lundy, their former home was renamed Cliff Bungalow, a rather drab title, but perhaps it was deemed inappropriate for the next occupant, Lundy's new vicar, the Rev. Swatridge, to be receiving mail addressed to the Palace.

Bramble Villa

A colonial-style corrugated iron bungalow was built on this site in 1893 by the Rev. Hudson Heaven, but the current version is a prefabricated cedar-wood replica, built on the mainland and shipped over in sections to replace its derelict predecessor in 1971. Its name was given by the last owner of Lundy as a reference to the dense thickets that engulfed the original villa's garden as it gradually fell into decline.

The building's first use was as an annexe to Millcombe House, which at times accommodated a husband-and-wife team of gardener and cook, visiting children and their nurse and, in addition, provided a study for the Rev. Heaven.

Bramble Villa was rebuilt with the initial intention of housing some of the many workers involved in the complex rebuilding and restoration schemes instigated by the Landmark Trust, but instead became home to Lundy's resident agent. The exterior has weathered beautifully and reflects prevailing weather conditions. It gleams bright in morning sun, but sullenly changes mood and blends anonymously into the background when its timbers become darkened by driving rain.

Government House

Government House blends so harmoniously with adjacent buildings in style and appearance that one could be forgiven for assuming it belonged to the same period, rather than being only a couple of decades old. Sympathetic design coupled with judicious use of reclaimed stone dressing from the partial demolition of a nearby house have created one of the most delightful residences available to rent on Lundy.

Originally built by the Landmark Trust to house whoever happened to be the island's resident agent, Government House occupies a wonderfully sheltered site at the head of Millcombe Valley. It is only surprising that no dwelling had been built there earlier. One reason might well be that it almost overlooks Millcombe House and such close proximity represented an intrusion of privacy.

This was just one of the many major projects undertaken by the Trust after it assumed control of Lundy's restoration. Many of those involved in construction and renovation were based in Bath and had to be flown out by helicopter to work in four-week shifts on the island.

The Old House

When first built by Sir John Borlase Warren, Lundy's owner from 1775 to 1781, the house consisted of twin towers standing either side of a single-storey section, retaining that form until altered and enlarged by William Heaven around 1838. He built an additional floor, thereby raising the central part to the level of the towers, and then roofed the entire dwelling. The house that stands today is very close to that version, as later additions have been demolished and the stone put to alternative use, notably during the construction of Government House.

Once the Heaven family had moved down to Millcombe House, the owner's residence became known as the Farmhouse and was used to accommodate occasional guests. Author Charles Kingsley used it as a base when gathering material for his book *Westward Ho!*

During the 1860s when the Lundy Granite Company flourished, several buildings were added to the nucleus of the Farmhouse, including a village store, bakery and a substantial dwelling that was then called the Big House. As tourism increased, this was combined with the farmhouse to form one large hotel in 1926.

The Old School

The vibrant blue corrugated iron sheeting of the Old School contrasts starkly with the softer, neutral-coloured granite of its village neighbours. Originally erected in 1886 to act as a Sunday school, the building was later internally partitioned to make it habitable. Thereafter it was used for staff accommodation or leased as a summer holiday house.

For the benefit of one of its earliest tenants in the 1920s, the lean-to kitchen and WC were added, but that particular lady, a Mrs Fotheringham, was asked to leave by island-owner Martin Harman after it was discovered that she had been posting completed income tax forms from the island. Although laudably conscientious, it was deemed she was setting a dangerous precedent and one contrary to Mr Harman's belief that Lundy should be entirely independent from any form of bureaucratic control from the mainland. In fact, it was not until 1974 that the Inland Revenue finally decided that Lundy islanders were not exempt from one of life's only two certainties. The Old School entered its literally most colourful period during the late 1940s when it was let to Colonel 'Tubby' Harrison, an affable gentleman whose generous hospitality resulted in the Old School becoming known as The Red Lion. After the colonel's death, the bungalow was leased to Arthur Scudamore, when it was given the bright blue livery it still wears today, along with the affectionate title of the 'Blue Bung'.

FUNCTIONAL LANDMARKS

Alton Station
Alton, Staffordshire

Alton Station stands proudly alongside the redundant railway it once served, a nostalgic link with an era when steam trains noisily puffed their way round rural Britain, prior to large sections of the network being axed in the mid 1960s. From its position deep in the Churnett Valley, the station is overlooked by the gaunt hilltop remains of Alton Castle, built in Gothic style for the fifteenth Earl of Salisbury around 1809. Behind the castle, the vast landscaped grounds of Alton Towers are now world famous as a leisure park, filled with spectacular rides attracting visitors from all over the country, most of whom arrive by road. Long before they were equipped with modern entertainment technology, Alton's dramatic gardens were a popular weekend escape from the industrial towns of the Potteries for workers and their families, deposited at the station by special excursion trains up to twelve carriages long. The station's attractive Italianate exterior is perfectly complemented by the decor and furnishings inside, which so perfectly reflect the quiet, elegance of the period.

Every building has a purpose of some kind, but Functional Landmarks have served a more practical use than simply being dwelling places. These restored and converted buildings cover a wide spectrum, ranging from farmhouses, mills, schools and an old station to, perhaps most significantly of all in terms of Landmark Trust history, a simple canal lock-keeper's cottage.

The birth and early days of the Industrial Revolution were milestones in our economic development, and the establishment of a canal network was one of the most important stages. Before the advent of railways, canals were widely used to transport goods and raw materials round the country. Many of the buildings that sprang up along towpaths were an integral part of the system, accommodating those responsible for running and maintaining the waterways. When, in this century, canals were no longer viable as a means of transport, many of these buildings began to be demolished at random. Indeed, it was the needless destruction of Thomas Telford's Junction House on the Shropshire Union Canal that instigated the formation of the Landmark Trust.

Identifying and saving decaying buildings from oblivion is both time-consuming and costly, generally beyond the means of private individuals and way down the list of priorities for councils. Had the Landmark Trust not been established, many of these unspectacular but important links with the past would have disappeared long ago.

There seems to be increased interest in rural history and industrial archaeology, manifested by farm and mill museums springing up all over the place; but very often these consist merely of a collection of artefacts. Staying in a Landmark that has been directly linked to a specific activity or industry is so much more rewarding than staring at pieces of machinery in glass cases. Not only does one get more of a feel for the period, but Landmark bookshelves are always stocked with a carefully researched collection for those who want to increase their understanding of a particular era.

Few of the buildings are lavishly furnished and those that were once inhabited are equipped in a manner that reflects the simple lifestyle of their original occupants. There are undoubtedly more comfortable and stylish Landmarks than those that follow in this chapter, but these represent an essential part of our social and economic history and should not be overlooked.

The New Inn
Peasenhall, Suffolk

Pilgrims were the first travellers who took to the roads of England in any numbers in the early Middle Ages, making arduous journeys to shrines such as Canterbury, or Walsingham in Norfolk. Those who needed refreshment and accommodation on the way sought refuge in monasteries, many of which set up simple hostelries as demand grew, even brewing their own ales on the premises until the Dissolution of the monasteries under Henry VIII in 1536 forced their closure. Several were subsequently run by private individuals and there are still pubs in England today that began trading in that way. Commerce was also increasing, particularly during the fifteenth century in regions involved in the thriving wool trade. Suffolk was certainly flourishing at that time and the New Inn was custom-built to cater for business travellers. The method of construction varied only slightly from that which would have been employed to build a house of similar stature. Most main halls would have had two sets of doors, one leading to private rooms used by the family in the high end and another to the servants' quarters, known as the low end. At the New Inn this system was retained,

but an additional wing extending back into the courtyard was added for accommodating guests. The inn also differed in that it had an extra large cellar used for brewing or storage of ales, stables, barns and haylofts to provide for horses and pack animals.

The central hall was still the focal point where travellers gathered round an open central fire, swapping stories or simply listening to reports from other parts of the region, such contact often being the only form of news gathering. Changes occurred over the centuries and, although part of the building was probably an inn until the eighteenth century, the remainder had been divided and turned into cottages and a shop. The building's medieval past was gradually hidden under fresh plaster, new ceilings and other additions, but the structure slowly fell into disrepair, leaving the whole complex derelict and awaiting demolition by the 1950s. Fortunately, the local council discovered something about the New Inn's more illustrious past and there was a happy ending in sight, involving architects from the Landmark Trust rather than bulldozers. The hall has been restored to its original glory.

Stockwell Farm
Old Radnor, Powys, Wales

Stockwell Farm has the unremarkable exterior of a solidly built stone farmhouse of indeterminate age, but architectural research has revealed sections of an interior dating back to around 1600. At that time, cows and humans would have been accommodated under one roof; a separate wing was probably added around a century later. The present front door opens directly into a dining room, furnished in traditional style with dresser, scrubbed table and stone-flagged floors.
Old Radnor Hill climbs sharply up to over 1,000 feet from directly behind the farmhouse, its summit allowing uninterrupted views to the wilderness of Radnor Forest. Although some sections are planted with conifers, the title relates to Norman times when a forest was an open stretch of land designated for hunting. No roads cross this bleak outcrop and it remains very much the domain of hardy mountain sheep.
The hamlet itself is very small, but it has a remarkable church possessing a wealth of detail, including what is thought to be Britain's oldest organ casing and a font fashioned from a huge chunk of rock that may once have been a Celtic altar stone.

Obriss Farm
Westerham, Kent

Obriss Farm is set in 160 acres of pasture and woodland, isolated in the soft Kentish countryside near Sevenoaks. Most of the land is leased and organically farmed, leaving the typical brick, tiled and timbered farmhouse for letting. As the house is still surrounded by its original range of outbuildings, there are often opportunities to observe farming practice at close hand, not least during early spring when the great barn is sometimes used as a lambing shed.
Perhaps of even greater interest is the revival of charcoal burning, a local tradition that largely died out through being too labour intensive, but now ironically enjoying a new lease of life following the great storms of 1987 that destroyed much of south-east England's tree population. Vast swathes of timber were felled by the hurricane, but the dead wood can still be put to good use, creating a home-grown rather than imported product to burn on our barbecues.
Obriss Farm generates a delightful atmosphere of pastoral tranquillity; Sir Winston Churchill also found solace in this corner of Kent – his house Chartwell is one of Obriss's near neighbours.

Manor Farm
Pulham Market, Norfolk

There are two distinctive smells in many of the older Landmarks: wax polish and the lingering sweetness of wood smoke from an open fire. Both were very much in evidence on my last visit to Manor Farm and I could quite happily have curled up on the sofa until gently reminded by the housekeeper that I had ten minutes left for photography before new guests arrived.

Pulham Market and neighbouring Pulham Mary have an abundance of fine old houses, the latter also possessing a very fine fifteenth-century church. Manor Farm is a later, Elizabethan farmhouse, acquired by the Landmark Trust in 1979 after the previous owners felt they were no longer able to provide the necessary amount of care to maintain the building. Thankfully, it was that same couple who had rescued the farmhouse back in 1948 when it was almost derelict, preventing it from being plundered for its antique oak beams and panels.

An eighteenth-century annexe on the end of the house looks out of place up against the main structure, but it has at least provided a place for a ground-floor kitchen and first-floor bathroom to be inserted, ensuring minimal intrusion into the original house, which has remained virtually unchanged.

Although now glazed on the outside, the windows of one small room still have the original sliding wood shutters in place and timberwork is very much to the fore throughout. Upstairs is a roller-coaster ride across rooms whose floors seem to tilt first one way then another, all made from planks of great width.

The quality of the fittings throughout suggest that the farmer who once occupied Manor Farm was well off and derived a decent income from the land, possibly supplemented by additional activities such as weaving, as Pulham cloth was acknowledged as a furnishing fabric of some quality. Manor Farm's exterior had been given a 'make-over'; an earlier ochre colourwash was replaced by subtle pink walls in a shade described on the National Trust paints colour card as 'ointment', offset by woodwork in 'cooking apple green'. However, such names are quite irrelevant as the result is outstandingly beautiful and perfectly complements the interior. If I were compiling a shortlist of Landmarks that truly reflected the style and atmosphere of rural England centuries ago, Manor Farm would be at the top.

Brinkburn Mill
Rothbury, Northumberland

The Augustinian monks who built Brinkburn Priory in 1135 chose their site well. Hidden away in a deep, isolated ravine carved by the River Coquet, the religious enclave was often overlooked by Scottish raiders on frequent sorties south of the border during the turbulent early Middle Ages.

It is unclear when the mill was first established, although it was certainly listed on an inventory of possessions made in 1536 when the priory was dissolved. There was some doubt as to whether the present building actually occupies the same site as the original, as it was unusual for a mill to have been downstream of a priory because sewage, effluent and kitchen waste would all have been discharged straight into the river. However, recent architectural evidence suggests there has always been a mill here. It comes as no surprise to discover that Turner included the mill in a painting dated 1830, as the Coquet is renowned as an excellent salmon river and the artist was a keen fisherman. His watercolour depicts the mill as a small humble structure, so it seems it was substantially enlarged and improved at a later date, possibly during the 1850s when the church was being restored.

Lock Cottage
Stoke Pound, Worcester, Worcestershire

The Worcester and Birmingham Canal formed an important trade link between the two cities when it was constructed during the early nineteenth century. Over half its 30-mile length was taken up by the fifty-eight locks needed to raise the canal up to Birmingham's higher altitude, the greatest concentration located at Tardebigge whose flight of thirty is Britain's longest.

The Landmark is a former lock-keeper's cottage that stands next to the towpath once used by horses to haul heavily laden barges, but now frequented by walkers, cyclists or those helping pleasure craft negotiate the lock system. The interior retains a plain, functional atmosphere, but undoubtedly offers a great deal more comfort than experienced by its original occupants.

Canals may be undergoing a new lease of life, but traditional, brightly painted narrow boats passing Lock Cottage will probably only be carrying holidaymakers, as inland waterway transport is a thing of the past. When our roads are clogged up with traffic, it is sad that canal and railway networks have been allowed to decline such an extent that they can no longer be considered a viable option.

The College
Week St Mary, Cornwall

Established in 1506, the College was one of the first schools founded by a woman, the wonderfully named Thomasine Bonaventure. Originally a native of the village, she apparently married and survived three husbands in London, all of whose property she inherited and subsequently gave to charity. Some of the funds were put into her own charitable institution, and the house that stands today is just one part of a larger collection of buildings that formed the school. Two granite features stand out in the College: a huge smoke-blackened fireplace in the living room and a substantial carved doorway, the detail of which is clearly visible, despite exposure to centuries of Cornish weather.

When setting up her school, Thomasine had also stipulated that the master in charge should offer prayers for her dead husbands. Such good intentions unfortunately led to the College's premature demise some forty years later. As it had acted as a chantry it was dissolved in accordance with Henry VIII's Act of Dissolution.

Although the village of Week St Mary may not be the most visually attractive, having been built up over the years using different styles and materials, there is ample compensation for any lack of ambience in its close proximity to the beaches and surfing havens of Bude and Widemouth Bay.

Sanders
Lettaford, Devon

Dartmoor is England's most southerly national park, renowned for its countless distinctive granite outcrops, or tors, eroded into weird hilltop sculptures. Despite its bleak, often inhospitable environment, it has been settled since prehistoric times and traces of those earliest settlements are still very much in evidence throughout the moor.

Lettaford is a perfect example of one of Dartmoor's later communities, a tiny farm hamlet hidden away down a narrow lane barely wide enough for vehicles. As a result of Lettaford's isolation, it has not attracted the attention of those who might seek to change or modernize, a situation further consolidated by the Landmark Trust, which has secured three of the most important buildings.

Agricultural life is represented by Sanders, a typical Devon longhouse probably built about 1500 to accommodate livestock and people under one roof and sharing a porched entrance. That part of the building that once housed animals remains empty and unconverted, while guests occupy the same rooms as generations of farmers and labourers, protected from harsh weather by thick granite walls and warmed by a large open fire.

The lane that leads to Lettaford goes no further so there is no traffic noise to intrude on a silence that has remained unbroken for centuries.

The Grammar School
Kirby Hill, Richmond, North Yorkshire

Kirby Hill is one of a line of small villages near the North Yorkshire – County Durham boundary, running parallel with the A66 trans-Pennine link from Scotch Corner to Penrith. To the south of the village are the open moors leading down to Swaledale and 'James Herriot country'. On a fine summer's afternoon, Kirby Hill's spacious village green could be considered light and airy, whereas a less polite description would be more appropriate when cold winds swirl in from the high hills.

The Grammar School is tucked away in one corner of the green, its rear windows facing on to the gravestones of the fourteenth-century parish church dedicated to St Peter and St Felix. The church's tall buttressed tower is a landmark for miles around.

The Catholic vicar of Kirby Hill, John Dakyn, was responsible for founding both the school and the trust that owned it in 1556. During the same period, he was an active participant in Mary I's campaign of religious persecution, ordering that a Protestant be burned at the stake in nearby Richmond for alleged heresy.

The Dakyn Trust is still active today, providing charity for those in need and educational grants for local children, although the school itself closed in 1957 after serving the community for 401 years. Wardens who administer the trust are still selected every two years using the same method instigated by Dakyn centuries ago. The names of six suitable local candidates are written on slips of paper, which are then encapsulated in balls of wax, rendering them waterproof. In a public ceremony, these are dropped into a large jar of water, which is stirred around with a shepherd's crook by the vicar; two balls are drawn from the jar. Those elected serve for two years, but the remaining four wax balls remain sealed in the jar kept in Dakyn's cupboard. Should a vacancy arise in the interim, another person is chosen using the same process.

The Landmark Trust was given a long lease on the Grammar School in 1973 and has repaired the ground-floor schoolroom for use as a village hall, or by visiting school parties on educational trips to the village. The upstairs accommodation once used by the master is now where Landmarkers stay, stone steps leading to the private first-floor entrance. A collection of old school books provides a poignant reminder of the past.

Beamsley Hospital
Nr Skipton, North Yorkshire

Hidden behind a row of stone cottages, the unusual circular building of Beamsley Hospital was originally founded in 1593 by the Countess of Cumberland, who was distressed at seeing so many old women having to beg on the streets of Skipton. Following the Dissolution of the monasteries around 1536, the poor were no longer able to seek help from religious institutions. Beamsley housed a small community almost continuously right up until the 1970s, when the advent of sheltered housing and other schemes reduced the need for institutions like this to care for the elderly.

Possibly based on the round churches of the Knights Templar, a centrally sited chapel ensured that the seven residents were constantly reminded of God's presence when leaving and entering their wedge shaped perimeter rooms.

Twentieth-century alterations had been made to provide small kitchens and bathrooms for the women, but all have been stripped out during restoration to return the hospital to its original form. The chapel is still in place, equipped with prayer and hymn books for any Landmark guests who may feel suitably moved on a Sunday morning.

34, High Street
Ironbridge, Shropshire

Unlike some properties where one is actually living inside a piece of history, spending time at 34, High Street makes one part of it. The Landmark at Ironbridge is located almost next to a milestone in Britain's industrial development, Abraham Darby's famous iron bridge. Spanning the wooded slopes of the Severn Gorge and erected in 1779, it was the world's first cast iron bridge and now forms just one part of the impressively designed Ironbridge Gorge Museum, a collection of sites recreating aspects of life as it was in Coalbrookdale at the birth of the Industrial Revolution. Separate areas are devoted to Coalport china, ceramic tiles and iron smelting. 34, High Street, overlooking the river bank, is a substantial square building that originally housed a grocery business. Street-level is now occupied by the Museum Trust shop, allowing parts of the upper floors to be divided to form two flats, one of which is for Landmark Trust guests. From their high vantage point, all rooms benefit from the same outlook across the gorge and, once the tourists have departed, Ironbridge's unique slice of heritage is all that remains in view.

Appleton Water Tower
Sandringham, Norfolk

Examples of functional buildings worth saving do not get any better than Appleton Water Tower, a classic piece of Victorian architecture that one could spend hours admiring. East Anglia is littered with water towers, mostly concrete obscenities that add nothing to the landscape, except concrete. Perhaps the only sad thing about Appleton is that, despite a hilltop site, surrounding trees prevent one from appreciating its graphic outline from a distance.

A water tower was originally commissioned following concerns over the quality of supply on the Sandringham Estate, no doubt prompted by the future Edward VII and his eldest son both contracting typhoid there within the space of three years. The first stone was laid in July 1877, but acrimony broke out shortly afterwards between a tenant farmer and the Prince of Wales over damage caused by construction traffic to a newly laid road, both parties claiming ownership and accusing the other of wilful damage to property.

Basic accommodation was provided for the custodian on the ground and first floors, while the second formed an elaborate viewing platform, often used by royal shooting parties. Frozen supplies in winter were never a problem as the resourceful engineers ran chimney flues from the caretaker's fires up through the centre of the main tank.

Appleton Water Tower is all about spiral staircases, spectacular views and the slightly unnerving experience of living in an octagon.

Danescombe Mine
Calstock, Cornwall

Sprawled along the Tamar's steep northern bank, Calstock was an important river port until the arrival of rail transport (a graceful twelve-arch viaduct still spans this now tranquil stretch of water). A narrow lane passes under one of the arches and runs alongside the riverbank before disappearing into a steep wooded valley containing overgrown relics of Cornwall's copper and arsenic mining industry.

Danescombe Mine was just one of many in the district exploiting rich copper deposits for a large part of the nineteenth century. When copper began to run out, many mines turned to arsenic production as a way of staying in business, responding to demand from America where it was used as a pesticide to protect cotton plants against the ravages of the boll-weevil. Much of the process was done by hand and those workers directly involved, whose skin had absorbed arsenic dust, were said to have glowed in the dark, exuding an eerie green phosphorescence.

The Landmark has been created in what was once the mine's engine house, which drove powerful rollers to crush ore-bearing rock. Danescombe does not provide luxury accommodation, but the surroundings and atmosphere more than make up for any shortcomings. Just a very short walk through the woods leads to the beautiful Tudor house at Cothele, now in the care of the National Trust. Most of its original furniture and tapestries still remain *in situ*, all lit naturally through leaded windows as no electricity supply has been installed.

Church Buildings and Gatehouses

Whiteford Temple
Nr Callington, Cornwall

When the Duchy of Cornwall gave Whiteford Temple to the Landmark Trust, it had a corrugated iron roof, an earth floor and was in use as a cattle shelter. An air of mystery surrounded the isolated building in terms of what function it had served when part of an estate established by Sir John Call towards the end of the eighteenth century. A former military engineer, Call married and retired to Cornwall at the age of 38 on the proceeds of a lucrative spell in India, but all that remains of his wealth is the Temple.

No records or details existed to help the Trust recreate what might have been, so a combination of guesswork and intuition has gone into the restoration. It is not even clear that the Temple was ever a place of worship. Small wings on either side of the Temple accommodate kitchen and bathroom, leaving the main area free to form a gracious living room. The Temple's stylish interior and bold, granite front make it a curious addition to a part of Cornwall normally associated with mining relics.

Although the buildings grouped together in this chapter vary enormously in size, style and origin, most remain linked by the common bond of being surviving fragments of once illustrious surroundings. Gatehouses that once guarded huge mansions or abbey entrances now overlook farm buildings, empty parkland or parish churches, while monastic ruins provide ample evidence of the nationwide network of magnificent religious architecture that fell to Henry VIII's commissioners during the Dissolution.

Of those ruins that have been saved, Warden Abbey is the most puzzling as so little has remained above ground, giving little indication of the quality of work that might have existed. It is perhaps ironic that the Cistercians followed the strictest monastic rules of all, yet their monasteries and churches displayed some of the country's finest Norman architecture. The substantial ruins of Fountains and Rievaulx Abbeys in Yorkshire bear testimony to the status achieved by the Order.

A quarter of all land in England was granted to the Church after the Conquest, a wealth manifested in the sumptuous architecture of many monastic churches. One only has to walk a few paces from the Abbey Gatehouse in Tewkesbury to study the opulence contained within the former abbey church to realize just how richly endowed the monastic orders were. They provided rich pickings for Henry VIII when he plundered their wealth, ordered the buildings to be pulled down and handed over much of their land to high-ranking officials, or sold it off cheaply to other local landowners.

While there is no evidence to suggest that Tixall Hall was built from the proceeds of monastic plunder, the gatehouse would have been typical of many built during that period: a bold statement designed to impress, at times providing an additional suite of rooms to house guests or a senior member of the household staff.

In strong contrast to the extravagances of mainstream religion, the humble chapels built by Nonconformists contained few frills. Their builders concentrated only on the need to provide a communal place of worship, which, in the case of many early Welsh chapels, had to be as remote as possible to avoid the persecution of the congregation.

Some Landmarks can be taken at face value, the buildings and their surroundings being as they were when originally completed, but others provide tantalizing glimpses into their former grandeur, where imagination is the only key to unlocking the past.

Langley Gatehouse
Acton Burnell, Shropshire

Langley Gatehouse is hidden deep in rolling countryside, looking across to the dramatic outline of the Wrekin, one of Shropshire's best-known hills, on which a beacon was lit to warn of the Spanish Armada's approach. The gatehouse is a real 'Jekyll and Hyde' building as it has two distinct characters. One side, now facing into a farmyard, is constructed entirely of stone, but the other, now overlooking empty fields, exhibits a most amazing kaleidoscope of timber framing. When the gatehouse was built in 1610 the positions were reversed, as the timber-framed frontage was then part of Langley Hall and would have been used to house guests or perhaps the steward.

Langley Hall was demolished in 1880 and natural decay was about to claim the gatehouse, which was on the point of collapse, but a joint project with English Heritage enabled Landmark to step in and rescue the failing building. Some of the rooms are panelled and the attic rooms have an interesting collection of beams surrounding the beds, some of which might be too close for comfort if one sits up too sharply.

Bromfield Priory Gatehouse
Nr Ludlow, Shropshire

Bromfield is typical of many buildings saved by the Landmark Trust, in so far as it was drawn to the Trust's attention by concerned members of the public who had observed its gradual decline. The estate owner had hoped to repair it himself, but had made only limited progress. Consequently, a lease was granted to the Trust in 1990.

The gatehouse was originally built in the fourteenth century to secure the entrance to a small Benedictine monastery built near the confluence of the Rivers Teme and Onny. When the monastery was dissolved in 1538, the gatehouse was used for a variety of purposes right up until the 1970s. The black and white half-timbered room above the original stone archway was not added until midway through the sixteenth century. One of its earliest recorded functions was as a village courtroom, used by the lord of the manor to settle local disputes. Records show this continued until 1770, after when it fell into disuse and decay.

A later lease of life came in 1836 when the gatehouse was enlarged and restored to act as the village school until 1895.

Tewkesbury Abbey Gatehouse
Tewkesbury, Gloucestershire

The former abbey church of St Mary the Virgin dominates Tewkesbury's flat water meadows where the River Avon joins the Severn. A bloody battle was fought here in 1471 during the Wars of the Roses, resulting in a Yorkist victory and the death of the seventeen-year-old Prince of Wales, whose body is buried under the abbey's choir.

A gatehouse was built about 1500 to guard the abbey precincts, and its single room over the arch is now cleverly converted into an atmospheric bed-sitting room. Maximum use has been made of the limited available space by encasing unsightly cooking and bathroom facilities in a gallery at one end, with steps leading up to an open sleeping area above.

The church is of cathedral proportions and was one of the few monastic churches to have survived the Dissolution intact, as sufficient funds were raised locally to buy the church from Henry VIII. The sheer beauty of the Romanesque nave and 132-foot tower, both exhibiting Norman work of the highest quality, are complemented by some of the finest medieval tombs in England. The exterior view of the abbey in front of its great west end is quite unforgettable.

As Tewkesbury is an ideal base from which to explore further afield into the Cotswolds, one could even contemplate spending time at both Abbey Gatehouse and the weavers' cottages in St Mary's Lane (see p. 43).

Shute Gatehouse
Nr Axminster, Devon

Thomas Witty's first Axminster carpet was completed on Midsummer's Day in 1755, and when subsequent ones were finished, church bells rang and the carpet was carried in procession to the church for blessing. Whether one ever found its way to Shute Barton is not known, but the house now in the care of the National Trust is only three miles away.

The house does not belong to any one period, as it has been added to over the years after being started around 1380. The gatehouse is thought to have been erected by William Pole after he bought Shute in 1560 and was altered again sometime during the mid-nineteenth century.

One of the outstanding features in the gatehouse is a Jacobean plaster ceiling, although it was imported from elsewhere during renovations by the Landmark Trust. Prior to the demolition of a house in Barnstaple during the 1930s, North Devon district council officers had the foresight to dismantle the ceiling in pieces and place it in store. The ceiling was offered to the Landmark Trust when it was restoring the gatehouse. Although slightly reluctant to introduce something into a building that was not part of the original fabric or design, Landmark decided that it could not turn down such an offer, particularly as the date of the ceiling was not far off that of the gatehouse.

Tixall Gatehouse
Tixall, Staffordshire

Mary, Queen of Scots spent two weeks at Tixall Hall in 1586, not as an honoured guest but as a prisoner of Elizabeth I. There are no traces left of the original house, which was demolished in 1927, and its gatehouse seemed destined for a similar fate. When the Landmark Trust arrived at Tixall in 1968, the gatehouse was in a very sorry state, lacking roof, floors and windows, and the walls were likely to succumb to gravity before long. As with many other apparently lost causes taken on by the Trust, it has been restored to its former glory and is now one of the most interesting places one could hope to stay.

Because the gatehouse was a shell, no real clues existed as to how it might have been laid out, although the number of fireplaces often provides an indication as to the number of main rooms. In recreating an interior for the gatehouse, the architects made full use of space in the four turrets, housing three bathrooms and two bedrooms in total. There is safe access on to the stone paved roof, offering far-reaching views over the valley of the River Sow down towards the magnificent house of Shugborough. Tixall's interior is very special, but to be up among the balustrades and turrets on a clear evening with only the stars for company is even more so.

Lynch Lodge
Alwalton, Peterborough, Cambridgeshire

There might be times when residents of
Alwalton would wish that all vehicles
using the nearby A1 dual carriageway
were as quiet as those developed by the
village's famous son, Henry Royce, of
Rolls Royce fame.

Lynch Lodge occupies a quiet corner near
the end of a cul-de-sac opposite the church
and vicarage and is only a very short walk
from the delightfully thatched post office,
which sells extremely good honey.

The tall, mellow stone Jacobean porch does
seem slightly out of place in both style and
colour, perhaps attributable to the fact that
it did not originate in Alwalton. The
building was originally part of a house in
Chesterton near Cambridge, which
belonged to the Dryden family and was
often used by the celebrated poet. The
house was demolished early in the
nineteenth century, but the porch was saved
and transported to its present location by
the Fitzwilliam family, who decided to use
it as a lodge house for the estate drive in
Milton Park.

Although the parish church is most
attractive, any visitors who choose to stay at
Lynch Lodge must brave the nearby centre
of Peterborough to see one of the country's
best-kept secrets – Peterborough Cathedral's
wonderful decorated ceiling.

Cawood Castle
Cawood, North Yorkshire

An inspiring building set within the rather
drab countryside to the north of Selby,
Cawood Castle became more of a palace
during the fourteenth century and was
home to seven Archbishops of York. The
gatehouse that forms the Landmark was
added by Cardinal Kemp sometime during
the following century and has a particularly
fine decorated bay window over the
entrance porch. Cawood received so many
royal visitors over the years that it became
known as the 'Windsor of the North'.
Monarchs who stayed at the palace included
Henry III, Edward I, Queen Isabella and
Henry VIII with temporary wife number
five Katherine Howard.

Although the palace itself had been partly
demolished after the Civil War, the
gatehouse functioned as a courtroom during
the eighteenth century, when a wider stone
staircase was added to supplement the more
difficult medieval spiral version. This
staircase only goes as far as the current first-
floor living room, so guests using the
gatehouse will need to negotiate a very steep
twisting flight to reach the bedroom.

It took some considerable time to free the
gatehouse from the constraints of
neighbouring buildings, but the land has
now been cleared to expose the palace's old
domestic wing, whose darker brickwork
makes an excellent contrast to the pale
stone gatehouse.

Warden Abbey
Old Warden, Bedfordshire

The flat Bedfordshire countryside surrounding Old Warden houses two very different kinds of relic. On one side of the village, the Shuttleworth Collection is famous for its veteran aircraft, whose fragile frames still take to the skies at weekends. Much older and arguably more intriguing are the remains of Warden Abbey, standing defiantly alone in the centre of a field. This small Tudor building is all that remains of a Cistercian monastery founded in 1135, a daughter house to the illustrious abbey at Rievaulx in North Yorkshire, whose ruins are one of the finest examples of England's great monasteries. Warden has not fared so well and was almost completely demolished during the Dissolution.

During the four centuries of its existence, the abbey obviously prospered. A magnificent mosaic pavement from its church is now in Bedford's museum, but very little else is known about other achievements during that time, although one secular contribution is well recorded: the Warden pear. Monks are renowned for their horticultural skills and the brothers at Warden cultivated a small cooking pear, used to make Warden pies, a dish

mentioned by William Shakespeare in his play *The Winter's Tale*.

When the end came for the abbey, it was not allowed to fall into picturesque ruins but demolished almost immediately. Most of the stone was sold off for other uses and at least 400 cart-loads were taken to Bedford to build a new gaol. Thereafter, possibly around 1552, a large red brick Tudor mansion was built on the site by the Gostwick family. This was eventually pulled down in 1790, but a short wing was left standing and that curious fragment is all that remains of Warden Abbey.

It must have been soundly built to have survived well into the twentieth century, as county records from 1912 described it as 'very ruinous'. The building that stands today is clearly Tudor, identified by the tall mullioned windows and wonderfully ornate chimney, but during restoration work it was realized that the north-west corner was a stone buttress from a medieval building and might well have formed part of an abbot's residence. In some ways it is interesting to learn about a building's past from old records, but even when few exist, as in the case of Warden Abbey, the pleasure of staying there is not diminished.

Woodspring Priory
Nr Weston-Super-Mare, North Somerset

It may well have been a bit of soul-cleansing that led to the formation of Woodspring Priory in 1210, dedicated to St Thomas the Martyr. William de Courtenay was a member of one of the West Country's best-known families, but dark deeds lingered in the past as his grandfather, Reginald FitzUrse, was one of the assassins of Thomas à Becket in Canterbury Cathedral. Woodspring Priory came into the care of the Landmark Trust when the National Trust purchased the whole Woodspring Estate as part of its campaign to preserve as much of Britain's valuable coastline as possible against inappropriate development. The priory buildings were very run down and needed a good deal of time and money spending on them.

For some strange reason, Woodspring did not suffer real physical damage at the time of the Dissolution and the church was turned into a farmhouse, complete with chimney stack poking up through the nave roof. When restoration began in 1969, the most pressing task was to secure the tower from imminent collapse. A tree trunk was embedded in one corner, roof timbers were rotten, lead gullies were leaking into the

building and a stone parapet was held up simply by twine and wire.

When the most urgent repairs were completed, the tower was repointed, but this proved to be a laborious task taking eighteen months. No less important, and not particularly pleasant, was the job of removing several tons of bird droppings that had accumulated over the delicate fan vaulting in the tower crossing. As there was no access from below, a window in the tower wall had to be removed and the waste taken out bit by bit in plastic bags, a process that took a week.

Two bedrooms and a sitting room now continue the nave's occupation, other rooms having been created from other parts of the priory including a section built in 1701 on the site of the prior's lodgings.

Both tower and infirmary are permanently open to the public, while Landmarkers' accommodation has private access. A simple museum has been created to exhibit old documents and photographs and other small relics found during restorations. This important project has resulted in the saving of two parts of our heritage: a lonely piece of coast and a now not-so-lonely monastic building.

Parish House
Baltonsborough, Somerset

Parish House directly overlooks the churchyard of St Dunstan, dedicated to England's first patron saint, who was Abbot of Glastonbury and Archbishop of Canterbury during the reign of Edgar in the tenth century.

What is unusual about the Landmark here is that it forms part of a building that has remained in the care and use of the parish since it was built around 1500. Rising costs of upkeep and repairs often lead to similar properties being transferred to private hands, but in the case of Baltonsborough the Landmark Trust has taken on its care, enabling the village to retain its interest. The ground floor is still the parish meeting room, adorned at one end by a huge fireplace, and the two principal rooms of the Landmark are directly above.

The main first-floor room was at one time divided by an oak partition, which has been retained to form one bedroom and a large living area, both under the same magnificent arch-brace roof timbers. One of the most striking things about the roof is the comparative lightness of the beams – similar houses usually have far more substantial support.

Baltonsborough is not far from the wonderfully atmospheric town of Glastonbury and even closer to Street, now known nationwide for its massive shoe-factory retail outlets.

Priest's House
Holcombe Rogus, Devon

If the Landmark in Holcombe Rogus had really been the priest's house, he would not have had to travel far to his place of work, as it is next to the church entrance. However, it would appear that the building should really have been endowed with the name of Church House, as it performed the function of both parish meeting place and village pub.

This was a common use and many similar buildings went on to become fully fledged public houses. Being associated with the church, such houses were linked with monks' for meeting the needs of travellers. Many of the West Country church houses that became inns originated as somewhere for the church building masons to eat, sleep and no doubt drown their sorrows on Saturday nights. The Priest's House had a kitchen for the provision of food and may have had its own small brewery, a frequent practice in medieval times.

Possibly because of its slightly claustrophobic position, the building has never really been put to another use or sold into private hands for alteration, but that at least has led to it remaining largely unaltered. Landmark has restored oak panelling where it might have been and relaid a stone floor. As several original windows have survived, the house may well look much as it did four centuries ago.

The Old Hall
Croscombe, Somerset

Croscombe is situated midway along a pleasant valley linking Shepton Mallet and Wells, the latter renowned for the stunning beauty of its Gothic cathedral. Although considerably more modest than its illustrious neighbour, Croscombe is blessed with a handsome parish church, which contains an unusually complete set of seventeenth-century fittings including box pews, canopied pulpit and a lofty screen. A little further up the steep hill, another place of worship can be identified by the one or two gravestones standing outside its main doorway, but there the similarity ends. What was once a Baptist chapel has been restored and is now a Landmark, resplendent in ochre-tinted limewash walls beneath a roof of glowing orange pantiles. The Old Hall had been used by Baptists from the early eighteenth century until the 1970s, by which time a combination of dwindling congregation and an east end near to collapse led to its abandonment. Fortunately, a West Country architect discovered the building by chance, temporarily stabilized the threatened section and persuaded the Baptists to sell the chapel. The Landmark Trust then became its saviour.

Such timely intervention was extremely fortuitous as it resulted in the preservation of a much older building than might have been assumed. The chapel had originally been the great hall of an early fifteenth-century manor house, no other parts of which have survived. Built by William Palton around 1410, the manor changed ownership several times through marriage or inheritance, but gradually decayed, having been split up and let to tenants by absentee landlords.

The hall was well cared for by the Baptists, who ensured that essential structural repairs were carried out, in addition to making several internal alterations. One item in the records worthy of note was the installation of a baptismal tank in 1824, eliminating the need for cold journeys down to the local river for ceremonies of total immersion. Although the hall now looks much as it might have done originally, complex structural operations had to be undertaken to secure the building's basic structure. Stainless steel rods were used to prevent the heavy roof from continuing to force weakened, unbuttressed walls apart, a task previously performed by the tie beams of a Victorian ceiling. That has been removed to expose the magnificent oak roof made up of four bays with five arch-braced trusses.

Tall, graceful windows are one of the chief delights of the hall, but for many visitors the star attraction becomes the Gurney Patent stove from Romsey Abbey. Lurking at one end like a malevolent black-finned dustbin, the stove generates an amount of heat quite disproportionate to its size, but it has a voracious appetite and seems to require almost constant attention. Feeding the Gurney can end up taking precedence over other planned activities, but nobody cares as it provides a good excuse to stay in and simply enjoy the Old Hall.

127

The Old Parsonage
Iffley, Oxfordshire

Despite being nearly swallowed up by the spreading mayhem of Oxford, the quiet corner of Iffley where the parish church and Old Parsonage stand together has that timeless feel reminiscent of many rural English villages. Those choosing to stay in the Old Parsonage will find a peaceful reminder of a more gentle age, a residence of some elegance and comfort that many will be reluctant to leave.

The atmosphere generated by some Landmarks is so special that just being around them is pleasure enough; intended sightseeing and itineraries seem somehow irrelevant.

The parsonage garden has an attractive mulberry tree in the centre of the lawn, which slopes down towards the River Thames. Indeed, a pleasant stroll along the towpath is by far the best way to get into Oxford.

Dark wood panelling lines the living room where one's attention is drawn to a gold inscription in bold Gothic lettering running round the room. Latin scholars will immediately feel at home, but lesser mortals may have to seek a translation in the history notes that are found in every property. The words of wisdom actually say: 'For we know that, if our

earthly house were destroyed, we have a building of God, a house not made with hands, eternal in the heavens.' How could one possibly argue with that?

The Old Parsonage is, in fact, semi-detached, the Landmark being an addition of around 1500 to the earlier rectory, which is still used in that capacity to serve the parish church of St Mary. Built towards the end of the twelfth century. Its west front exterior is rich in beakhead and zig-zag carving, while the interior contains two equally elaborately decorated arches. Most of the rooms have been altered at some stage, notably when some Victorian restoration took place at the end of the nineteenth century, but unlike many fine medieval country churches that have been ruined during 'renovation' by overzealous architects from that period, the Old Parsonage has been sensitively handled and remains unspoilt.

The second-floor bedroom offers a view over to the 'dreaming spires' of Oxford's colleges, particularly fine during winter when the prospect is enhanced by lack of foliage on the trees.

Ty Capel
Rhiwddolion, nr Betws-y-coed,
Gwynedd, Wales

Much of the appeal of
Landmarks is that they are well
off the beaten track, so for
anyone seeking a base from
which to explore Snowdonia, Ty
Capel provides an exhilarating
alternative to the plethora of
guest houses and gift shops in
Betws-y-coed. Straddling the
course of an old Roman road,
Rhiwddolion was originally a
small slate-quarrying community
of about 150, and Ty Capel
acted as village chapel and
school. The miners and their
families are long gone, leaving
behind a handful of buildings in
an enclave of pasture surrounded
by the dark green forestry that
blankets much of upland Wales.
The converted chapel, which has
three beds on a first-floor
balcony, is a solid stone building,
well insulated by the varnished
pine boarding lining its walls, but
only accessible on foot. Before
locating the path's starting point
and abandoning the car, one first
has to negotiate successfully a
maze of forest roads. Failure to
follow Landmark's detailed
instructions to the letter,
especially as night falls, could
result in a less than cordial
atmosphere developing
between driver and navigator
as the same tree stump is passed
for the fifth time.

Maesyronen Chapel
Glasbury-on-Wye, Powys,
Wales

The small isolated chapel of
Maesyronen is a perfectly
preserved example of an early
Nonconformist meeting house.
Prior to Methodism becoming an
accepted part of Welsh life,
gatherings were held in secrecy to
avoid persecution. Although the
chapel was established in 1696,
shortly after the Act of Tolerance
granted greater freedom of
worship, the barn that was
converted to accommodate the
chapel was probably used as a
venue for earlier gatherings.
As the Methodist Revival
gathered pace during the
eighteenth century, shaking
Wales like an emotional
earthquake, chapel services
developed into occasions of
drama and almost theatrical
passion. Preachers delivered
powerful, emotive sermons,
rousing congregations to respond
with hymn singing that became a
religious and social ritual, a
source of sheer physical
enjoyment that continued
through the tradition of Welsh
choral singing.
The Landmark is, in fact, a
cottage added on to the side of
the chapel at a slightly later date,
probably some time before 1750,
and is as humble as its neighbour,
recreating the atmosphere of life
in rural Wales centuries ago.

FOLLIES AND CURIOSITIES

The Pineapple
Stirling, Central Scotland

Of all the follies that grace the parklands of Britain's large country houses, the Pineapple at Dunmore must surely rank as one of the most audacious, both in design and execution. One really needs to see it in person to appreciate fully the complexity and quality of stonework that has gone into making such an accurate replica. Many will have seen photographs of it as a result of its ownership by the National Trust for Scotland, but perhaps very few realize that the Landmark Trust has a lease on the Pineapple and it can therefore be enjoyed as a place to stay.

Lord Dunmore was responsible for its creation around 1777, seemingly upon returning from America after being expelled from his post as Governor of

The landed gentry of the eighteenth and nineteenth centuries who ventured abroad on the 'grand tour' were obviously impressed by many of the sights encountered on their travels; Greece, Rome and Egypt proved particularly fertile inspirations for new schemes and ideas. Many an English architect must have dreaded the return of a patron from such an expedition, wondering what complex creations they might be asked to build. During this period, English country estates blossomed with Greek temples, Roman arches and even replicas of pyramids from ancient Egypt.

The use of follies changed around the mid-eighteenth century when 'natural' landscaping became popular, spearheaded by such famous designers as 'Capability' Brown, Charles Bridgeman and William Kent, whose new approach can still be admired in locations around the country, most notably Claremont Landscape Garden in Surrey. The new aesthetic made more use of trees and natural features, but in a carefully orchestrated fashion that harnessed the effects of light and shade to create environments where a judiciously placed structure would act as a visual magnet.

Of course, not all follies were merely attractive sculptures. Rich industrialists delighted in their new landscaped surroundings and were anxious to show them off to visitors whenever possible. Architecturally elaborate pavilions and banqueting houses were built in the grounds and used as surprise venues for lavish summer lunch parties and picnics, to be happened upon 'by accident' during conducted tours of the estate. The Banqueting House at Gibside is a typical example.

The majority of follies and curiosities taken on by the Landmark Trust date back to an era when almost anyone who had the means at his disposal could indulge himself in a trifle of architectural whimsy. One hardly dare contemplate the response of a council planning committee chairman today if presented with an application to erect a pigsty in the form of a classical Greek temple, or to adorn an existing property with a large stone replica of a tropical fruit.

There are those who consider that many modern buildings can already be classed as follies, but whether they will feature as such in some future Landmark Trust handbook, time alone will tell.

Virginia. During his time there, he must have noticed a local tradition whereby sailors would impale a pineapple on their gatepost to announce a safe return home. Dunmore obviously had a keen sense of humour and made a similar gesture, albeit a trifle more permanently. Perhaps we should be thankful that Virginians did not use apples as a symbol – a stone Granny Smith would have singularly less appeal.

The guest rooms have been created from gardeners' bothies built either side of the folly, although one slight drawback is that sleeping and living accommodation are separated by the Pineapple itself and there is no way through. Consequently, access from one to the other is via outside doors, so producing hot breakfast in bed could be a challenge.

Laughton Place
Laughton, East Sussex

Isolated and apparently marooned on the lonely reclaimed marshland of Glynde Levels, the red brick watchtower of Laughton Place is the sole survivor of a moated manor house, extensively remodelled on earlier buildings by William Pelham in 1534. This somewhat forlorn remnant of past grandeur contrasts starkly with the present-day opulence of one of Laughton's nearest neighbours, the world-famous opera house of Glyndebourne, which is less than two miles away.

There had been a manor, or estate, at Laughton long before the sixteenth-century version to which the tower belonged. It had been owned by an Earl Godwin prior to the Norman Conquest of 1066, and thereafter became attached to larger Sussex estates granted to barons or knights by the king, although titles and land underwent frequent changes of ownership through marriage, inheritance or by incumbents simply falling out of favour.

Accounting records dating from the late thirteenth century indicate that the manor at that time consisted of an aisled hall, hall chamber, kitchen, chapel and solar, all contained within a moat crossed by four bridges. The current tower was probably designed to fulfil a dual role, incorporating a solar room into the more functional purpose of lookout post.

Pelham family involvement with Laughton can be traced back to 1401, when it was

leased for £60 per annum by the Constable of Pevensey Castle, Sir John Pelham, from the manor's owner, the Countess of Oxford. However, it was a different John Pelham who made his mark in history when fighting for Edward the Black Prince at the Battle of Poitiers in 1356. Pelham was one of the knights who had accepted the French king's surrender and received the monarch's belt buckle as a tangible token of his direct involvement. The buckle symbol was thereafter adopted as a family emblem and can be seen in the tower today, featured on original terracotta mouldings that surround door and window frames. Although some have remained intact, several sections had broken up and have been cleverly restored by joining fragments together using glass.

The task of saving Laughton Place began in 1978 and represented Landmark's toughest restoration project so far. The main threat came from huge cracks on either side of the tower, which were repaired using a grid of steel tie bars. The gaping cavities were then made good with new bricks set into place using special lime mortar, which offers greater flexibility.

Visitors who stay in the tower have to negotiate a seemingly endless, tight spiral staircase from ground-floor kitchen to upper-floor bedrooms, no mean feat after a celebratory dinner, but there is at least a stout rope to assist any faltering ascent.

The Bath House
Walton, Warwickshire

According to some eighteenth-century medical opinion, the taking of cold baths was vital for the maintenance of good health, so to keep up with prevailing fashion the landed gentry set about building bath houses in or around their country houses. This new trend coincided with the practice of 'natural' landscaping by such designers as 'Capability' Brown, with their penchant for temples, follies, pavilions and other decorative buildings.

Bath houses quickly became a popular addition to estates, and the one at Walton was built for Sir Charles Mordaunt in 1748. Some way detached from the main house, it stands surrounded by dark woodland but has an open frontage looking out over sloping fields. The bath chamber itself is constructed from roughly hewn stone, in plain contrast to the smooth façade of the upper room used by bathers to recover from their ordeal. Decoration in the salon is quite whimsical. The walls are festooned with a combination of plaster icicles and garlands of seashells, originally the work of Mary Delany who was perhaps better known for her cut-out paper flower pictures, many of which are housed in the British Museum.

Vandalism had caused enormous damage to the Bath House, but the interior has been fully restored during a four-year programme and underground springs still gurgle happily up into the bath.

St Winifred's Well
Woolston, Shropshire

Pilgrims occasionally visit the Shropshire St Winifred's Well, but the majority seeking comfort from the seventh-century Welsh saint's healing powers are more likely to be found taking the waters at her shrine further north at Holywell, known as the 'Lourdes of Wales'. Most legends have been embellished by the passage of time, but it seems that St Winifred was beheaded by a Prince Caradoc for resisting his advances, a spring gushing up from the spot where her head fell. The medieval half-timbered Landmark was originally a chapel erected over the well that appeared at Woolston when her body rested overnight on its passage to Shrewsbury Abbey.

A spring emerges from under the building into a large stone bath created to allow bathing in the waters, a practice that was stopped during the eighteenth century because of excessively unruly behaviour by the public. Flowing away from the retaining bath, the waters form a pool surrounded by damp, drooping vegetation. The rich green plants are enlivened by yellow clusters of marsh marigolds in early summer.

St Winifred's Well later acted as a courthouse before it was lived in as a cottage, and its interior is dominated by huge, exposed roof timbers that appear capable of supporting a building several times larger.

The East Banqueting House
*Chipping Campden,
Gloucestershire*

Chipping Campden prospered from the wool trade that enriched many other Cotswold towns and villages during the Middle Ages and this small market town of golden limestone houses retains several impressive buildings from that era. One of the town's chief benefactors was Sir Baptist Hicks, commemorated by a monument in the magnificent Perpendicular 'wool' church at one end of the town. Immediately next to the church entrance, two small ogee-domed lodges form the entrance to what were once the grounds of Campden Manor, Sir Baptist's sumptuous house begun in 1613. Much of Sir Baptist's work was destroyed during the Civil War when the manor was burnt down by Royalist forces in 1645. One of the best views of what remains is from one of the roads leading out of Chipping Campden, across meadows bought by the National Trust to preserve the surroundings of the church. The East Banqueting House stands alone with a single, forlorn fragment of the original house visible in the background. This wonderfully ornate structure has been leased from the owner, a descendant of Sir Baptist, to be restored and converted for use as a Landmark.

The building has three floors and was built on the edge of the main garden terrace, but only the upper storey has direct access from the garden. From the double doors that open out from the dining room, one can see the remnant of the main house and it was from there that the family would stroll after dinner, taking further refreshment in the banqueting house while admiring the views across open fields. One of the entrance lodges provides additional accommodation, but all guests must enter the grounds on foot, something that enhances the experience of visiting the East Banqueting House. From one's approach along a grassy path, it is easy to visualize the gardens as laid out originally, as some of the raised walks are still visible. Sir Baptist Hicks's contribution to Chipping Campden can still be admired in the pillared Jacobean market hall, erected two years before his death in 1627, and the picturesque row of almshouses in Church Street that he also endowed. There are many other ancient buildings worthy of note, not least the fourteenth-century home of wool merchant William Grevel and the Woolstaplers' Hall, which now houses a local museum.

The Prospect Tower
Belmont Park, Faversham, Kent

General Harris's small flint tower was not easily converted into living accommodation, and a great deal of ingenuity was required to find space for everything. It was built a few years after the general bought Belmont Park Estate in 1801, a purchase funded from the proceeds of a successful military campaign in India that endowed him with not only ast wealth, but also the title Lord Harris of Seringapatam.

At that time, such ornamental buildings were fairly common and the tower may well have been chosen from an existing range, rather than being custom built. As its name implies, the Prospect Tower was used as a vantage point from which to enjoy the surrounding countryside, providing an agreeable stroll from the main house and a venue for summer family picnics. This type of building was also often used aesthetically by garden designers as a focal point, and the Prospect Tower was readily incorporated into Belmont Park's revised landscape plans. Immediate descendants made little use of Belmont until, in 1872, the fourth Lord Harris decided to create a cricket pitch on open land next to the tower and it was pressed into service as a pavilion, the Belmont XI taking on quite formidable opponents at county level.

Restoration has involved replacing all floors and ceilings, although some of the original floorboards have been reused, stud marks from cricket boots still pitting their surface.

Luttrell's Tower
Eaglehurst, Southampton, Hampshire

Despite the approach to Luttrell's Tower from Southampton being not particularly inspiring, power station and vast oil refineries are quickly forgotten as a final bumpy track opens out into the landscaped grounds of Eaglehurst House, in which stands the Georgian folly of Luttrell's Tower. This delightful building is almost on the shore of the Solent, facing directly towards the Isle of Wight and the world-famous yachting centre of Cowes.

Temple Luttrell was a Member of Parliament, but one reputed to have indulged in smuggling activities, a suggestion possibly borne out by the presence of a tunnel from the tower's basement leading directly on to the beach. Following his death in Paris in 1803, Luttrell's folly passed to his brother-in-law, Lord Cavan, who had commanded British troops in Egypt. He added a souvenir of the campaign to the base of the tower, thought to be part of a statue of Rameses II. Landmark has arranged the interior so that living space occupies the second floor, while ensuring that views of the deep-water shipping channel into Southampton are not obscured by surrounding trees.

A quite unexpectedly ornate flight of stairs with gates to match leads directly down on to the tree-lined foreshore. Eccentric Welsh architect Sir Clough Williams-Ellis designed the seaward entrance and might well have thought Luttrell's Tower would fit comfortably into his eclectic collection of buildings at Portmeirion.

The Coop House
Netherby, nr Longtown,
Cumbria

Coops are normally associated with the keeping of poultry, but the term also refers to devices used for trapping salmon and the Coop House stands overlooking the site of a stone weir once used for fishing on the River Esk. The twin-turreted summer house was built in the grounds of Netherby Hall towards the end of the eighteenth century by Dr Robert Graham, both as an adornment to his estate and somewhere from which to enjoy the river.
In more recent times, the folly was used to house estate workers, but its isolated location led to it being abandoned in 1936, becoming gradually more decrepit until taken on by the Trust some 50 years later. A long track leading to the Coop House has been reinstated, yet the building and its setting are best appreciated from the opposite bank, reached by a narrow suspension bridge. This also provides access to the estate church of St Andrew, built around the same time as the summer house and enjoying a wonderful setting on the river bank.
Netherby Hall featured in the novels of Sir Walter Scott, notably *Marmion*, in which the Graham family heiress elopes with young Lochinvar.

Swarkestone Pavilion
Nr Ticknall, Derbyshire

The sixteenth-century hall belonging to the Harpur family was demolished over 200 years ago, leaving this most elegant building to stand alone near the banks of the River Trent. Commissioned in 1631 by Sir John Harpur to celebrate his marriage, it has now been fully restored from a roofless shell to its original configuration. In common with similar buildings of that period, the Pavilion's principal room is on the first floor. In this case it affords a clear view of activities taking place in the walled enclosure below. Various theories have been put forward regarding likely events held here, ranging from bear baiting to jousting, but evidence gleaned from estate records indicates a more genteel use. Bowling was a popular sport and to have one's own bowling green was something of a status symbol.
Anyone contemplating staying in the Pavilion needs to know that the bedroom is on the first floor of one tower and the bathroom is on the second floor of the other. Consequently, night-time ablutions will involve a flight of stairs and a trip across the roof terrace – absolutely marvellous on bright starry summer nights, but less so in winter.

The Banqueting House
Gibside, nr Rowland's Gill, County Durham

The landscape of the Derwent Valley, once ravaged by the huge scars of open cast coal mining, has gradually been reclaimed and restored to its original state. Very much the same could be said about the Banqueting House at Gibside, for many years a silent observer of desecrated hillsides, during which time it, too, decayed, a pathetic reminder of past splendour. Accurate restoration of such ruins is a task requiring infinite patience, detailed research through archive material and a large slice of luck. All were needed to save Gibside, not least the good fortune that rewarded a meticulous search of the undergrowth and leaf mould surrounding the building for fallen fragments of masonry. Much of the missing stone was recovered and, with the help of old photographs and drawings, the architectural jigsaw was eventually completed. Delicate plaster decoration on internal walls had also suffered badly during the years of neglect, but enough remained *in situ* to allow accurate restoration by skilled modern craftsmen.

The Great Room measured 32 feet across and had mirrors at either end to create the optical illusion that meant, in the words of a nineteenth-century observer, 'the company when seated appears almost endless in

length'. Decoration inside the salon consisted of intricate papier mâché designs to walls and ceiling, but those were not replaced; a new dado rail copied from an original in the bedroom was used instead.

Although small in stature, the Banqueting House is regarded as a valuable example of Gothic design, and its architect, Daniel Garret, a particularly fine exponent. Three soaring pinnacles grace a frontage that faces down a long grass slope to an octagonal pool, one of many features in the expanses of Gibside's landscaped gardens, certain parts of which are slowly being restored.

The Gibside Estate was inherited by George Bowes in 1722, who, up until his death in 1760, transformed the parkland and added several important buildings, including the Banqueting House in 1746. Two of the most important elements in the gardens are the Avenue and the Chapel, both donated to the National Trust in 1965.

The Chapel was commissioned by Bowes to be completed within six years of his death, but the interior was not finished until 1812. A half-mile avenue of oak trees leads away from the Palladian chapel, passing the ruins of the Orangery and Gibside Hall itself, towards a 140-foot column of British Liberty, just visible from the Banqueting House above a dark screen of conifers.

The Château
Gate Burton, Lincolnshire

The River Trent winds sluggishly behind the Château, but fortuitous positioning and an abundance of trees keep the river obscured from the Landmark. The Trent is not at its most attractive on this stretch and is further blighted by the cooling towers of a power station. Fortunately, the view both from the Château and across parkland to it is probably much as it was when designed in 1747 by John Platt, who undertook the work at the surprising age of nineteen and exhibited a design sense that belied his years.

Although it appears to be a substantial structure from a distance, detailed inspection shows the folly to be quite small inside and space is at a premium. When originally commissioned as a weekend retreat for a lawyer from nearby Gainsborough, it may not have required all the facilities demanded by a twentieth-century clientele. The left-hand wing is a staircase, while the one on the right contains bed spaces on both floors. One hesitates to use the word 'bedroom' as there is precious little, more a question of open the door and jump in. By locating other facilities on the ground floor, maximum space has been allocated to the living room above, and its spaciousness is increased by a high domed ceiling.

When the housekeeper's young daughter once enquired if her mother was going to the Château, she was unable to pronounce the French word so called it 'the doll's house on the hill'. Not a bad description, really.

The House of Correction
Folkingham, Lincolnshire

There are certain connotations relating to the name of this Landmark that are perhaps best left unexplored, or for anyone still puzzled, unexplained. Houses of correction were local prisons where petty criminals served relatively short sentences, but hard labour and spartan living conditions combined to form a harsh regime, especially for those convicted of the once-serious offence of idleness.

At one time the Lincolnshire village of Folkingham was an important place in the county, being a noted coaching halt and seat for the Quarter Sessions Court. The Greyhound Inn still occupies a prominent position in the broad market place, but the dramatic stone façade of the prison is all that remains of the justice system.

The House of Correction was built on its present site in 1808 to replace an earlier institution in the village that had, ironically, been condemned as unfit by a prisons inspector. The austere gatehouse was added seventeen years later, apparently to act as a deterrent against reoffending.

Up to seventy inmates were once housed inside the prison, which finally closed in 1878. Bricks from the perimeter walls and other buildings were used to erect cottages around the compound and a larger house where the Landmark now stands. That Georgian building was partly demolished so that the gatehouse could be returned to something approaching its original layout. The final part of restoration involved reinstalling a section of prison wall either side of the gatehouse so that the frontage is once more seen in context.

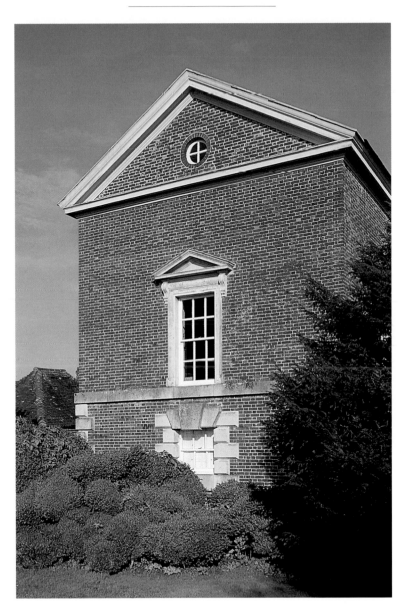

Fox Hall
Charlton, West Sussex

Charlton is a pleasant but unremarkable village on the Sussex Downs to the north of Chichester, where the local pub name, The Fox, provides the only obvious clue to earlier history. The Duke of Monmouth founded the Charlton Hunt during the 1670s and it rapidly became the focus for those in the local nobility who rode to hounds. Many were drawn by its reputation for fast, unrelenting cross-country gallops and convivial company when the day's sport was over.

As it was common practice to stay down in Charlton, members of the hunt commissioned Lord Burlington to design them a building that could be used as a kind of gentleman's dining club, and this became the original Fox Hall. Not to be outdone by his fellow sportsmen, the Duke of Richmond built his own hunting retreat, a small Palladian brick building next to the cobbled stable yard, and it is this that now forms the Landmark. It somehow inherited the name after the hunt was moved to nearby Goodwood House around 1750, the original Fox Hall disappearing soon after.

The building's bland exterior contrasts with a greater degree of opulence and style inside. The most interesting features are the ornate, gilded alcove that contained the duke's bed and a curious device set over the fireplace. At first glance it appears to be either a clock or a barometer, but it is, in fact, a wind-direction indicator, supplying information vital in planning the day's hunting.

The Library
Stevenstone, Great Torrington, Devon

Standing in almost perfect symmetry, the Library and Orangery are early eighteenth-century remnants of Stevenstone. The house itself underwent a final rebuilding in 1870 but has not survived, and a handful of other dwellings now make up the small community reached by a narrow lane running through a patchwork of fields.

The Library may have originally been conceived as a banqueting house, but there are no explanations as to why, or when, it was converted into a library. Not all Landmarks come with a fully detailed history, which somehow increases their fascination, inviting all who stay in them to use imagination in solving the mystery still shrouding some buildings. The Trust ensures that every property is equipped with detailed historical and architectural information, so there is usually ample scope for individual research.

When the buildings were purchased in 1978, the Library had been a house for some time, internally divided and the elegant loggia closed in. The main room has been opened up again and is rather a grand affair, with a somewhat formal atmosphere.

The Pigsty
Robin Hood's Bay, North Yorkshire

The eccentricity of Englishmen is renowned the world over, a characteristic perfectly highlighted by the Pigsty. Why house your pigs in a common-or-garden sty when they can just as easily be accommodated in a Greek temple? The setting makes it even more incongruous, perched at the top of a field overlooking the North Yorkshire coast near the old smuggling village of Robin Hood's Bay. There is no documented reason why Squire Barry of Fyling Hall should have gone to such extremes, but the mere fact that some people are prepared to set themselves against established practice can only serve to enrich our environment.

It is fortunate that the Landmark Trust existed, because the last owners would have had no real option but to let the building fall into decline, there not being many other uses for a classical pigsty. Simple accommodation is provided for two people and the Landmark is perfectly placed for exploration of this dramatic section of coastline.

Robin Hood's Bay has become something of a tourist trap during the summer, but the long sweeping bay linking it to Ravenscar provides a far more tranquil alternative.

The Swiss Cottage
Endsleigh, nr Milton Abbot, Devon

Devon and Cornwall are divided by the natural boundary created by the River Tamar. Rising only six miles away from the North Cornish coast, it virtually bisects the south-western peninsular *en route* to journey's end in the English Channel at Plymouth. Its rapid dash south is halted abruptly midway between Launceston and Tavistock by high outcrops of hard rock, causing the river to meander slowly round the impervious obstructions in deep, serpentine loops. The natural beauty of this stretch of the Tamar attracted the attention of landscape artists including Turner, its setting also proving irresistible to Georgina, Duchess of Bedford, who chose the site as the perfect setting for a new house around the turn of the eighteenth century.

The services of renowned architect Sir Jeffrey Wyatville and landscape designer Humphrey Repton were enlisted to bring the project to fruition, a task that included not only designing the main house, but also introducing other more fanciful buildings into the deeply wooded estate.

One of the most important of those was Swiss Cottage, its location appropriately spectacular. This extraordinary creation from 1815, reflecting a nineteenth-century passion for anything Alpine, perches precipitously on a ledge high above the river. The minutely observed detail on some of the exterior timberwork is quite extraordinary, and apparently its furnishings were completely Swiss in style and content, even down to the crockery.

Following structural restoration work after its purchase of Swiss Cottage in 1977, the Landmark Trust has ensured that, while internal fittings maintain the intended effect, content is toned down from the over-obsessive original, but visitors will definitely still find a cuckoo clock on the wall.

The first-floor veranda, once used for hosting shooting party lunches, provides a wonderful place to sit and do absolutely nothing, except listen. Every sound from the river valley far below seems amplified, so that even the faintest birdsong pierces the deep stillness with astounding clarity. (See also p. 40.)

The Egyptian House
Penzance, Cornwall

England's most westerly town has been popular with tourists since the Regency period, attracted by its mild climate and beautiful scenery. Town centre and harbour are linked by Chapel Street, a narrow thoroughfare containing many interesting eighteenth- and nineteenth-century buildings, including the bizarre frontage of the Egyptian House. It is something of a shame that the street is so narrow, as it prevents a full appreciation of this extraordinary building – the pavement opposite is often congested with sightseers straining to get a decent view of the upper levels.

Although motifs and designs from ancient Egypt may seem a curious form of decoration, it was a style that enjoyed some popularity following the French occupation of Egypt in 1798, which allowed architects greater access to monuments and other art forms.

This particular example was built for John Lavin in 1835 as a shopfront from which he sold geological specimens. Cornwall is rich in minerals and local mining activity would have produced many fossils for collectors, in addition to pebbles, rocks and stones gathered from beaches. Its construction may seem an unnecessary extravagance, but we are the richer for it, as few shop owners today would consider such an extrovert act, or even if they did, planning consent would be highly unlikely.

Directly across the road is the Union Hotel, which boasts a place in history, for it was there that Nelson's victory and death at the Battle of Trafalgar were first proclaimed.

INFORMATION FROM THE LANDMARK TRUST

The Landmark Trust is an independent conservation charity, founded in 1965, which rescues and restores buildings of historic and architectural importance, and then gives them new life and a future by making them available for holidays.

The Landmark Trust Handbook contains descriptions, histories, photographs and plans of all 165 Landmarks currently available as self-catering holiday accommodation, and explains the Trust's approach to conservation.

If you would like to buy a copy of the current Handbook (price refundable against your first booking), to make a booking, or to learn more about the work of the Landmark Trust, please telephone 01628 825925.

The Landmark Trust, Shottesbrooke, Maidenhead, Berkshire SL6 3SW, England

Registered Charity number 243312

Map of Landmarks, including those in Italy and the Channel Islands

LANDMARK LOGBOOKS

The accommodation industry uses a variety of methods to monitor the service it provides, usually by inviting guest comment via questionnaires or visitors' books. The Landmark Trust is no different in that respect, and an appropriate form is available in each property to highlight any problems encountered during a stay.

Where the Landmark Trust differs, however, is that it provides a forum for visitors to communicate their feelings and observations about a building and its environment to their successors through the medium of the logbook, a large hardback volume whose contents often span a period of years.

Consequently, visitors to each Landmark can share the experiences and emotions of their predecessors and add their own thoughts for the benefit of those who follow. Perhaps the most surprising aspect of the logbook is that it is never abused: there is a total absence of fatuous comment, sarcasm or ill-judged humour likely to cause offence. Completing an entry in the logbook can become a daunting proposition as the time for departure draws ever closer, and the desire to write something meaningful and different often becomes an overwhelming obsession. Because the pages are fixed, there is no opportunity for correcting mistakes, it has to be right first time. On the last night of a holiday, many Landmark living rooms resemble an author's study, with piles of discarded rough notes littering the floor as the deadline approaches.

Logbooks contain an astounding variety of material, varying from seriously considered architectural observations, through to children's accounts of holiday activities that would merit inclusion in any Enid Blyton *Famous Five* adventure. Seasoned Landmarkers make straight for the logbook when visiting somewhere for the first time, as they know it will contain the most important information of all – an infallible, unbiased guide to the area's best pubs and restaurants compiled by discerning consumers with no vested interests.

Perhaps the most overwhelming impression one gets from reading through logbooks is the sense of happiness and pleasure generated by spending time in a Landmark. Television is replaced by a carefully stocked bookshelf, an often frustratingly difficult jigsaw, a selection of games, but perhaps most importantly, by people rediscovering the art of conversation and just how much there is to talk about.

Here is a selection of entries taken from the logbooks of properties that appear in this book:

'A toad guards the steps by the side gate and the garden is alive with wild animals and birds: we saw a deer on the lawn one evening.'

'Much time was spent on top viewing the countryside through binoculars, watching the sun set and looking at the stars on a clear night.'
(APPLETON WATER TOWER)

'The nearest to Florence you get in England, with stunning views all the way up to the trees on the hills.'

'The Abbey Square was like an Italian piazza.'
(MARSHAL WADE'S HOUSE, BATH)

'We put the children in the dungeons, which they enjoyed.'

'A medieval atmosphere has been achieved without the discomfort of the period.'
(THE BATH TOWER)

'We found lots and lots to do and never strayed outside a five-mile radius from the house. Super walks and we managed to wangle a go in a coracle one evening.'
(CHURCH COTTAGE)

'We have played hide and seek, treasure hunts, rested on the lawn, threatened children with the cellar, ignored the outside world and fallen in love with Field House.'
(FIELD HOUSE)

'I found a bread and butter slug, it looked positively revolting.'
(FORT CLONQUE)

'How charming to find, behind the grand portico, something so elegant and snug.'

'Anyone who doesn't love their stay here needs locking up.'
(HOUSE OF CORRECTION)

'Saw the departure of HMS Battleaxe, dipped the Union flag, but she was ready for us and answered before ours was fully at the dip.'
(KINGSWEAR CASTLE)

'Every time we come indoors, the smell of wood smoke (and hot cross buns) makes my nose feel very pleased for the rest of me.'

'On with the jigsaw!'
(LYNCH LODGE)

'Opened our Christmas stockings to the atmospheric sound of carols filtering through the wall from the chapel.'

'Our dog had the best holiday a dog could have.'
(MAESYRONEN CHAPEL)

'Games and talk happily replaced the goggle box.'

'November, fish stew on the roof for Sunday lunch.'
(MARTELLO TOWER)

'The experience of living in such a building is so much more rewarding than merely visiting.'

'What a folly – only staying for three nights.'

'Farewell, old fruit.'
(THE PINEAPPLE)

'The pubs in Cynwyd are probably open, even if they look shut.'

'You can't really appreciate the Hall without the smell and light of the fire.'
(PLAS UCHAF)

'We came to Ty Capel with the idea of using it as a base to explore North Wales. It exercised its magic on us too and North Wales went unexplored.'

'To my surprise, I discovered that I actually liked walking.'
(TY CAPEL)

'We have found Stockwell Farm charming... we would love to come again, but it's a long way from Adelaide.'

'We have enjoyed the farm and the insight it gives one into the lives of our ancestors.'
(STOCKWELL FARM)

'If you enjoy beautiful countryside and incredible silence, then we think you will enjoy Tower Hill Lodge, as we have done.'
(TOWER HILL LODGE)

'We climbed the stairs and the cathedral became ours for a week – choirs rehearsing evensong, the doves, the laughter of children on the green, the sound of cricket, bells ringing the changes... just listen.'

'Even on the short journey from bedroom to bathroom I could not resist a detour to make sure the view was still there.'
(THE WARDROBE)

PHOTOGRAPHING LANDMARKS

The quality of prevailing light is paramount to creating good architectural photographs; shooting one's chosen subject in ideal conditions can transform what might have been an otherwise mediocre effort into a stunning picture. Therein lies the rub: being in the right place at the right time to take advantage of good light. Improved weather forecasting systems allow one to make a reasonably informed judgement on which part of the country is likely to have the best weather at any given time, so in theory, one should be able to plan accordingly. In practice, however, it is unbelievably frustrating to drive 250 miles on the promise of a clear interlude, to be faced with leaden skies producing a flat light, devoid of any character and totally useless. There are no magic tricks, filters or lenses that can do much to improve or enhance a typically dull British day to create worthwhile results.

Shadows and textures are an integral part of creating a good photograph; it is not enough merely to show the setting and size of a building. Using sufficiently atmospheric light should enable the viewer almost to feel the roughness of stone, count every blade of straw in a thatch and trace the grain patterns in timber beams. These effects are easiest to achieve in the early morning or late afternoon when light angles are low, directionally strong and have an added warmth that is useful for adding a tinge of colour to stark, whitewashed walls.

Summer is the worst time of year for architectural photography, as the sun rises high and spends much of the day directly overhead, lighting rooftops but little else, and trees are covered in foliage that often obscures vital parts of a building. If one is trying to catch soft early morning light, it could mean photographing around 6 a.m. or earlier, when people are still in bed with curtains drawn, a niggling detail that can make an otherwise attractive picture unsightly.

Autumn, winter and spring are potentially better because, although days are shorter and weather less predictable, the sun maintains a lower arc and so produces shadow and texture for much of the day, while trees are either stripped of leaves or form a background of rich autumnal colour. Skies contribute a great deal to a photograph, but they cannot really be planned for – one of my favourite combinations is a brightly sunlit building set against dark storm clouds. Dramatic photographs are often purely a matter of luck, of being able to capitalize on a situation that may last for a matter of seconds. It only takes one brief shaft of light to create a moment of magic.

It may seem quite ridiculous that split-second timing should matter when photographing a static object, but there were numerous occasions during the work for this book when success or failure hinged on one fleeting opportunity. The most stressful situations always seemed to occur the furthest distance away from home, when failure would have meant an awfully long return journey for a reshoot.

The most exciting aspect of photography is when things go as planned, such as creeping out of a hotel in the dark before dawn one frosty autumn morning to photograph the Pineapple, knowing that only a strong sunrise would light it to perfection and being rewarded by just those conditions. Any regrets about missing breakfast or any other meals are quickly dispelled by the euphoria of getting a good photograph (adrenalin is a very acceptable substitute for food).

All the pictures in this book were taken on 35 mm equipment, using an Olympus OM4Ti camera with lenses ranging from 24 mm to 200 mm; but for this particular assignment, the most important of all was a 35 mm 'shift lens'. This essential piece of equipment enables one to use a small format camera, but still achieve a degree of perspective control usually only associated with technical plate cameras.

Fuji Velvia 50 ASA slide film was used throughout, its slow speed necessitating the use of a sturdy tripod. Any interior photographs used only available light. Some required very long exposures, but by not introducing an artificial source one is able to retain a sense of a room's original and intended atmosphere.

A brief glimpse at the Landmark location map confirms how spread out the properties are, often in deep rural settings and almost impossible to find. Saturdays became absolute nightmares as they were changeover days and the only opportunity I had to take any interior photographs. Planning a schedule to fit in as many as possible between the hours of 11 a.m. and 4 p.m. was a logistical exercise that would have taxed the best military planners.

The fickle nature of our climate makes working outdoors an unpredictable business, but the rewards can be great when conditions are right, requiring a combination of patience, intuition and luck. I think completing this book has used up my reserves of all three. But being able to photograph so many historical buildings all over Britain that might now have been mere rubble had it not been for the Landmark Trust has been an exciting and rewarding challenge.

ALPHABETICAL LISTING OF LANDMARKS

Properties without a page number are not included in this book